BUDDHIST STUDIES
IN THE PEOPLE'S REPUBLIC
OF CHINA

Frontispiece. Juaji Wawa, Good luck spirit, meditating on a Buddhist Lotus, paper cut out, Shaanxi Province.

Asian Spirituality, Tendai Studies Series

BUDDHIST STUDIES IN THE PEOPLE'S REPUBLIC OF CHINA

1990-1991

Translated and edited by
Michael R. Saso

Tendai Education Foundation • Honolulu

© 1992 by Michael Saso

All Rights Reserved

Printed in the United States of America

ISBN 0-8248-1464-9

Camera-ready copy was prepared by the author

The paper used in this publication meets the minimum requirements of American National Standard for Information Sciences—Permanence of Paper for Printed Library Materials ANSI Z39.48-1984

Distributed by
University of Hawaii Press
2840 Kolowalu Street
Honolulu, Hawaii 96822

TABLE OF CONTENTS

Acknowledgements......................vi

Introduction..........................vii

Shenxiu and the Northern School of Zen

by Ren Jiyu.........................1

The Multi-ethnic Character of Chinese Buddhism

by Du Jiwen.........................22

Zhuangzi's Thought and the Spread of Buddhism

by Cai Dahua........................70

The Theory of Buddhist Spiritual Realms and Chinese Art Imagery

by Jiang Shuzhuo....................102

References..........................139

ACKNOWLEDGEMENTS

The editor would like to thank the staff of the editorial board, the Chinese Academy of Social Sciences, for the opportunity to translate and edit the articles appearing in this volume, especially Ma Jisen, Lei Ruoping, Liu Hui, Wu Jie, Bruce Doar, and Penny Barrett. Baima Wangyal, Nima Jaloteki, and other scholars of the Academy of Ethnology (Nationalties) continue to support the project for forthcoming publications.

I am especially grateful to the Rev. Ara Ryokan and the generous monks and nuns of Tendai Buddhism in Japan who helped make this second publication in the Tendai Educational series possible. Finally, recognition is due to Lucy Aono, Jan Heavenridge, and the staff of UH Press for the layout and preparation of the cover and the published text. Further titles in preparation for the series include studies of Tibetan Buddhism, Mongolian Shaman, and the customs of SE and SW China.

INTRODUCTION

The re-affirmation of the Freedom of Religion clause in the constitution of the People's Republic of China after 1979 brought about a rennaissance of Religious Studies, built on the work of Asian and Western trained Chinese scholars. Recent research in religious studies in the Chinese Academy of Social Sciences in Beijing, provincial branches of the Academy including Guizhou, Yunnan, and Xining, and religious studies programs attached to philosophy departments have produced a number of significant studies published in modern China.

The Journal of the Chinese Academy of Social Sciences (CASS) has translated and published a modest selection of these articles, mostly chosen from historical or theoretical studies in the Beijing area, or from related institutions nearby. Four such studies have been selected here for separate publication by the Tendai Educational Foundation of Hawaii, due to the interest and relevance these articles have to Buddhist dialogue abroad. The articles are as follows:

1. Ren Jiyu, director of the National Library in Beijing, in "Shenxiu and Northern Chan Buddhism," shows from recently discovered manuscripts that the teachings of Shenxiu and the northern school of Chan Buddhism did not differ significantly from Huineng's southern school of Chan. Differences occured after the death of the two great masters. A selection of texts attributed to Shenxiu found along the Yellow River as far as Dunhuang in the west are used to prove the hypothesis. Ren Jiyu is the former head of the CASS Center for the Study of World Religions.

2. Du Jiwen's "National Ethnic Minorities and Chinese Buddhism," shows that with the exception of Zhiyi, the founder of Tiantai Buddhism, all of the great thinkers of Chinese Buddhism between the 2nd and 8th centuries were of non-Han origin. By careful analysis of canonical texts, Du Jiwen shows that in fact the

intellectual movements of medieval China were the result of the interaction between the Han and "ethnic minorities." China's great thinkers of this period were in fact not Chinese. Du Jiwen is a senior Professor of CASS.

3. Cai Dahua, (Honan Academy of Social Sciences) in "Zhuangzi and the Sinification of Buddhism" analyze the stages of Buddhist teachings of Tiantai and Huayen, and the attitudes towards nature and "emptiness" of Chan, finding a closer resemblance to the Zhuangzi than to ideas with a clear Indian origin. To demonstrate the point, various passages from the Zhuangzi are read in synoptic comparison with Buddhist texts.

4. Jiang Shuzhuo, (Jinan University) in "Buddhist Realms and Chinese Art Imagery," explores the theories of the Buddha nature, Buddha realm, and Chan emptiness, which had a deep effect on Chinese artists, poets, and their work. The author cites passages from various dynastic artists and poets to demonstrate how Buddhist imagery effected art and poetry. The use of black ink on white paper, supporting Madhyamika emptiness, the place of the emotions and intuition in artistic creation, and meanings that goes beyond the limitation of words, are among the ideas discussed by the author.

The four articles translated here give a glimpse of the wealth of intellectual discussion found in relatively unknown Chinese sources today. Taoism, Islam, Christianity, and non-Han cultures of southwest China are among the topics found in recent PRC publications. The following studies are meant to encourage further dialogue between Chinese scholars in religious studies with their counterparts outside of China. (See the comment of Du Jiwen, pg. 24 below). Dialogue is made possible by the openness of scholars to the wealth of meaning in the Buddhist context.

                                        Michael Saso
                                        Honolulu, May, 1992

SHEN XIU AND THE NORTHERN SCHOOL OF ZEN

by Ren Jiyu

Chan (Zen) is a form of Buddhism that is special to China. Not only does India not have this kind of a sect, even within the Buddhist movements of China it holds a very special place.

A majority of scholars in this field hold that after the (fifth) patriarch Hong Ren, Chan (Zen) split into two separate schools: the southern school, represented by Hui Neng, and the northern school led by Shen Xiu. As the Chinese saying has it, "the South to Neng, the north to Xiu." The southern school of Zen became very popular, and its writings spread far and wide. The northern school on the other hand had only a few noted masters, and except for a few stone inscriptions and fragments, its writings are not found in complete systematized treatises. If we use the writings of the southern Zen school as a basis for our discussion, the writings of the northern school seem rather light and skimpy, as if they had not quite reached the level of earlier Zen masters. The most obvious example is the famous story told in the Platform Sutra, the chapter concerning the transmission of dharma.

In this famous passage, the fifth patriarch Hung Ren before his death suggested a theme for his disciples to respond to, asking who could best explain Zen teachings. Shen Xiu responded:

> The body is a Bodhi tree, the mind a mirror bright,
> Continually polish them, lest a speck of dust alight.

Hui Neng, when he heard Shen Xiu's reply, felt it was incorrect, and responded with his own verse:

> Originally there was no Bodhi tree,
> Nor was there a stand for the mirror.
> If originally there was nothing,
> Whereon can the dust fall?

These two verses, narrated in the *Platform Sutra*, as with so many of the myths related by the southern Zen school, try to establish the superiority of the southern style Zen over the north. I (and others) have shown in separate studies that the text is most probably spurious. The two poems found in the sutra are later creations of the followers of Hui Neng.[1] Leaving aside the controversies surrounding the credibility of the text, let us discuss the Zen practice taught by Shen Xiu.[2]

Shen Xiu (605-706) was named Li. He was born in Yushi county, Bian Zhou prefecture, Henan Province. He went to Twin Peak mountain in Qi prefecture (Hubei) where he received a Chan transmission from Master (Hong) Ren. A bright Chan (Zen) light, he broke from the way of words, destroyed the works of the mind, and did not publish any writings. After this he dwelt in Jade Spring (Yu Quan) monastery, Jing Zhou prefecture (Hubei Prov). In the first year of Da Zu (701), he was called to Luoyang, Eastern capital of the T'ang Dynasty, where he accompanied the Empress in her travels between the two capitals, (Luoyang and Changan) as a teacher (of Buddhism).

The Empress Wu asked master Shen Xiu what school the doctrine he taught came from. He answered, "From the East Mountain Dharma Path" (Dongshan Famen).
Question: "What sutra does it depend upon?"
Answer: "Manjusri's version of The Prajnaparamita Sutra, the Ekakarma samadhi" (the single act enlightenment, i.e., the one act of realizing that the nature of all Buddhas is the same).

The Empress Wu said: "In cultivating the way, nothing is better than the East Mountain Dharma path." It was because Shen Xiu was one of Hong Ren's disciples that the Empress said this....

Shen Xiu was more than 100 years old when he died, leaving the triple character *Qu Qu Zhi* as his last testament. He was honored with the posthumous title *Datong* (Great Universal) Chan master.[3]

One of the ten great disciples of Hong Ren, Shen Xiu's doctrines caused a great sensation in Luoyang and Chang An, earning him fame throughout the country. Zong Mi (780-841) felt that he should be listed with the *Xiwang xiuxin* (quelling the imagination and perfecting the mind) school. This sort of distinction seems reasonable, since concepts such as "perfecting the mind" (xiuxin) and "mind is the source of all dharmas" appear as an important part of Shen Xiu's teachings. They are consistent with the techniques attributed to Bodhidharma, such as purifying the mind from the intrusion of sensory data, in order to keep the mind quiet and pure.

The works of Shen Xiu himself seem to have been lost. However, the Tong dynasty monk Hui Lin in his *Yiqiejing Yinyi* (The pronunciation and meaning of the Ekayana) lists the *Guan Xin Lun* (On Contemplating the Mind) as a work of Shen Xiu. A manuscript entitled *Guan Xin Lun*, was found at Dunhuang. The basic ideas of this document have been taken as representative of the Shen Xiu school.

There was, regretfully, a lengthy period during the Tong dynasty when the teachings of Shen Xiu's school were deprecated, distorted and suppressed by the followers of Hui Neng. We must rely on sources such as the stone inscriptions listed in the *Datong (Shen Xiu) Chan Master Steles* of Chang Yue, for a description of the school's teachings:

> Concentrate the mind (nien) to stop the thinking process (xiang); be firm, hold the mind. When beginning, distinguish the worldly from the pure; once enlightened, do not distinguish before and after. Before Samadhi, close out sensory objects; after enlightening wisdom, all things are Tathagata. Hold Lankavatara (Sutra) as the basic teaching.

The above introduction of Chang Yue does not give sufficient detail in describing Shen Xiu's basic teachings. As the leader of the northern Chan school, there must have been some unique points powerful enough to win over a large group of followers. Besides the *Guan Xin Lun*, there are other documents, including the *Jue Guan Lun*, attributed to Boddhidharma, surviving in the Dunhuang collection. These texts can be used to establish the basic teachings of the northern school.[4]

The Chan school claims that as one of its characteristics it does not rely on the written word (buli wenzi). Thus, among the various texts which bear the same title, there is a great variation, even divergence in wording and length of the manuscript. The teachers of the various sects elaborate their own insights into the basic teachings of Chan in such a way that only their divergence seems to be the unifying element.

The method that we use to study the Chan (Zen) school, therefore, must be different from the way we would study, for example, the Fa Xiang school of Chinese Yogacara. In the case of the Fa Xiang school, the terms can and must be clearly defined, and are not open to a wide interpretative reading. In the case of Chan literature, on the contrary, one cannot delve solely into the meaning of individual statements, but must understand the meaning of the phrase in the context of the whole. Only by following the methods of the Chan school can its basic meaning be understood.

Progress has been made in analyzing the manuscripts of the *Wu Xin Lun, Guan Xin Lun,* and *Jue Guan Lun* in such a way that the founding and the teachings of the Northern school can be better understood. Here are some examples taken from the *Wu Xin Lun* (On No Mind):

> It is as if one were to see to the end of the day, and still see not, because in the end there was no mind to see.
> It is as if hearing all day to the end of the day, still one hears not, because in the end there was no mind to hear.

It is as if one feels all day to the end of the day, and yet
feels not, because in the end there was no mind to feel.
It is as if one knows all to the end of the day, and still
knows not, because in the end there was no mind to know.
For no mind is indeed true mind.
True mind is indeed no mind.
Question: Now what should be done within the mind by
way of cultivation?
Answer: In encountering all things realize that there is no
mind, this is the only practice. There
is no other practice than extinguishing mind.
Therefore know that no mind is everything;
Extinguishing (mind) is the same as no mind.
The disciple on hearing this achieved sudden enlightenment. He understood that there is nothing outside of mind, and no mind outside of things. By quelling both mind's action and rest, he was aware from within the self. He was rid of all doubts and freed from all obstacles.[5]

The doctrine of "No Mind" is taught to sweep away any attachment to sentient things, and any images of them in the mind. It is a method used in Mahayana Buddhism to teach people not to cling to external things, or their images. The doctrine of No Mind does not deny existence, nor does it propose that reality is empty or void. Its aim is simply to teach people not to let their minds be attached to things or dwell on mental images. Only then can one experience a "true mind."

Let my mind not be attached to giving or taking,
nor be taken up with keeping or breaking the laws;
Neither swallow insults, nor injure and kill;
Neither make great mental effort, nor be lazy at work;
Chan is not for enlightenment, nor to distract the mind;
Neither be filled with wisdom nor obtuse and dimwitted;
Let no thoughts of heaven arise, or hell fill the mind.
Be not filled with compassion or ridden with hate,

Neither seek a clear mind, nor let poison fill the heart,
Neither benefit from stealing, or fear being robbed.[6]

The absence or extinction of mind consists in not giving rise to any kind of thought. I.e., it teaches people in daily life not to calculate gain or loss, not to judge others as right or wrong. The idea of not calculating loss or gain, right or wrong means in fact to transcend affirming or denying, loss or gain. The inability to free the heart-mind from worldly cares makes it equally impossible to transcend the mundane which includes both pleasure and suffering. The text continues:

> Sorrow is sorrow only in the mind,
> Pleasure too is born in our mind;
> If forgetfulness is born in the mind,
> How can there be sorrow or pleasure?
> There are words that are written,
> Such as life and death.
> If there were no letters or words,
> It would be named "Nirvana" (annihilate written words);
> There are words that are spoken,
> Words such as life and death.
> If words were not spoken,
> It would be named "Nirvana." (Annihilate spoken words).
> There is cultivation and learning,
> It is called life and death;
> If there were no cultivation and learning,
> It would be named "Nirvana."
> There is wisdom and intuition.
> It is called life and death.
> If there were no wisdom and intuition,
> It would be named "Nirvana."

The text again says:

> To cut away suffering is called life and death;
> Not to cut away suffering is called Nirvana.
> To look for liberation is called life and death;

Not to look for liberation is called Nirvana.
To look for Nirvana is called life and death;
Not to look for Nirvana is called Nirvana.
To detest the world is called life and death.
Not to detest the world is called Nirvana.
To take joy in Mahayana is life and death.
Not to take joy in Mahayana is Nirvana.[7]

The Northern School of Chan holds that of all the forms of wisdom, no mind is the highest. The *Vimalakirti Nirdesa* sutra says that non-Buddhists are won over by promoting the (way of) no heart, mind, feelings or perception. The *Fa Gu Jing* (Dharma Drum Sutra) teaches that if one knows that there is no mind that can be attained, no Dharma, no sin or blessing, no life, death, or nirvana, that in the end all things cannot be attained, then "cannot attain" also cannot be attained.[8]

As for the problem of the nature of mind, Shen Xiu's school advocates the following methods to quell the mind and bring about the cessation of illusions:

Q. What is meant by "mind," and "quelling the mind?"
A. Do not force the mind to be alert or at rest;
   This is what is called "to quell the mind."
Q. If one does not think with the mind, with what does one think?
A. When there is thought, then the mind exists.
   When there is mind, then the Dao (Way) is false;
   When there is no mind, then the Dao is true.
   Whenever something is attained, then there is illusion;
   There is nothing for the sage to attain,
   So there is no illusion.
   No mind is no thing; non thing is natural (tian) truth.
   Natural truth is the Great Way.[9]

The meaning of extinguishing the mind:

Q. For all things thought is illusion; how eliminate it?

A. If one sees illusions, and sees them eliminated,
One is still fettered by illusion.
Q. As for the term sage, what Dharma must be cast off, and what Dharmas attained, to be a sage?
A. A sage neither cuts off or attains Dharma.
Q. Not cutting off or attaining anything, how is the sage different from an ordinary person?
A. They are not the same. All ordinary people think that They cut away some things, and attain others. Ordinary folk have things to attain. The sage has nothing.
Q. How are attainment and non-attainment different?
A. For the ordinary, attainment is an illusion. Because it is illusion, "same" and "different" are argued. When there is no illusion, there is no difference.
Q. Then if there is no difference, why have the title sage?
A. Both "ordinary" and "sage" are terms. In the middle way (n.b.. Madhyamika, *zhonglun*) there is no duality, and thus no distinction. *Sunya* (emptiness) then is the basic way (Dao, Margha).
Q. Is the Buddha then Sunya (empty)?
A. Yes (thus)!
Q. Then should the sage teach sentient beings to envision the Empty, instead of ordering them to think of Buddha?
A. For simple sentient beings, the sage teaches chanting to Buddha; for those in the way, he teaches contemplation on the Buddhakaya (the physical Buddha), seeing Buddha as if present. The *shixiang* (conditioned reality), the empty, and *wuxiang* unconditioned reality (that which is phenomenal, the empty, and the non-phenomenal) are one and the same.

Zhan Ran (711-782), of the Tiantai school, from Jingxi (in Zhejiang Province) taught the theory that even non-sentient beings have the Buddha nature (*Wu xing yu xing*). This theory was widely praised in Buddhist circles of the time, as a great advance in the doctrine of Buddha nature. At almost the same time the Chan school too brought forth such a doctrine:

> Q. Does the Dao only reside in beings who have a soul (ling), or is it also to be found in grass and trees?
>
> A. (by Ru Li): There is no where that Dao does not dwell.
>
> Q. If Dao penetrates everywhere, why is it not a crime to kill grass and trees, as well as man?
>
> A. Whether or not an act is a crime is usually a matter of feelings and convention, not in accord with true Dao (Dharma). It is because people do not attain true principles, that they hold to the illusion of "my own" body. To kill is a mental concept; the mind bound to Karma (deeds) is that which says "crime." It is because grass and trees don't have feelings that they are in accord with Dao. Because they have not established an "I" (ego), the person who kills them does not consider it to be a crime. Whatever lacks self-being (ego, "I"), conforms with Dao. What looks like grass and trees, is therefore to be cut down like grass and trees. Thus Manjusri once pointed his sword at Gautama, Angu (a Shivite convert) pointed a knife at the Buddha. All this is in accord with the Dao, and proves that what is non-arising (not born) does not know illusory change nor empty non-being, and so does not dispute whether it is a crime or not.[10]

The questions proposed in the above narration are all taken from the standpoint of ontology, while the answers invariably take the epistemological stance "no mind" (judgment) and its attainment. The questioner presses on with his problems further, and asks:

> Q. If all this time grass and trees were one with the Way, why do the sutras never say that they can become Buddhas, but only record that humans can do so?

A. The sutras not only mention humans, they also mention grass and trees. E.g., "Even the smallest grain of dust contains Dharma." And in another place: "All Dharma is the Tathagata; all sentient beings are Tathagata. The Tathagata has no duality, no distinction."[11]

The above passages make it abundantly clear that all dharma, i.e., everything that exists, manifests the Buddha nature, and that the Buddha nature shines forth in all existing things. This is the Chan version of the doctrine that non-sentient beings have the Buddha nature. We are not concerned here with the problem of whether Tiantai or Chan Buddhism originated the theory. When thinkers reached a given stage in the theoretical understanding of the world, similar questions and answers manifested themselves throughout China, reflecting the contemporary evolution of ontological philosophy. Such questions could not have been found in pre-Qin, or Prior and Later Han thinkers. The development of human knowledge brought such a response.

In order to destroy the illusion of an Atman (separate ego), the Theravada tradition analyzes the body as a conglomerate of the five skandhas (1. *rupa* five senses, 2. *vedana* act of sensation, 3. *sanjna* mind as forming concepts, 4. *samskara* mind as making judging good and bad, and 5. *vijnana* mind as discriminating self from things and affairs). The Mahayana tradition carries the process of breaking from Dharma (mind) a step further, by teaching people not to be attached to the written word of the scripture or its interpretation. The Buddhist scriptures teach that its followers should obey the five precepts (Not to kill, steal, have illicit sex, lie, or drink alcohol). The Northern school of Zen responds to each of these rules as follows:
On killing:
> Q. Because of the law of causation, is it sometimes permissible to kill a living thing?
> A. A wild fire burns mountains, violent winds fell trees, falling cliffs crush beasts, flooding waters drown

insects. The mind that distinguishes this process, like all humans is involved in killing. The mind that is irresolute, that sees life and death and dwells on it, is in the state of *antara-bhava* halfway between, a mind not extinguished. If you are such a person, then even an ant's life influences your destiny.

On stealing:

> Q. Because of the law of cause and effect, is stealing ever allowed?
>
> A. The bee sips honey from the flower, the sparrow pecks rice, the cow chews beans, and the horse eats hay. If you don't see self as other, then you can appropriate even a mountain for yourself. If you do, (see self distinct), then you are the slave of needles and leaves.

On illicit sex:

> Q. Because of the law of cause and effect, are immoral acts sometimes allowed?
>
> A. Heaven lies over earth, Yin joins with yang, the latrine is filled with urine from above, the valley is irrigated by water gushing up from springs. When the mind is thus, it is without obstacles wherever it goes. By distinguishing life from the realm of passion, then even intercourse with one's wife can be defiling.

On lying:

> Q. Because of the law of cause and effect, can one lie?
>
> A. Speak without a subject, talk with no mind, let sound be like a bell, and breath like wind. If the mind is like this, then neither Daoism or Buddhism exist. If the mind is not so, then even to speak of the Buddha is a lie.

On drinking:

> Q. When sober, where is drunkeness?
>
> A. It is just like turning the hand about. When you see that the hand is turning, don't ask where the hand is.

Another response:

Being drunk is not being sober; being sober is not being drunk. However, in drunkeness there is soberness, that is, being drunk is not being not sober.

The Northern School of Zen also teaches that the (five) basic rules of Buddhism are to be swept away as illusions.

Q. Can the person who drinks wine, eats meat, and gives in to the five passions, attain the way of the Buddha?
A. If mind focuses on non-being, who does right or wrong?
Q. What is meant by the Buddha's Dharma way?
A. The mind knows there is no Dharma, this is Buddha's way.
Q. What is the Tathagata storehouse?
A. To realize that one's mind is but empty form and dust, thus assuring that images do not arise this is the Tathagata storehouse.

Mahayana Buddhism teaches the six shores or crossings (i.e., six parameters, *paramitas*, 1) *dana*, giving; 2) *sila*, keeping the five rules; 3) *ksanti*, patience when insulted; 4) *virya*, zeal for practice; 5) *dhyana*, Zen meditation, and 6) *prajna*, wisdom), while Theravada Buddhism promotes the three basic doctrines (sila rules, samadhi concentration, and prajna wisdom). The Sat-paramita (six parameters) are six paths or practices to reach the other shore, ie, to cast off illusion and attain realization. The *Sunya* (Madhyamika or Middle Path) school teaches that wisdom is the greatest of the six paramitas, and does not give as much weight to the other five practices. The Mahayana theory of the six paramita emphasizes that all Dharma paths are empty, and seeks to eradicate all kinds of form, name, or image from the mind. Thus (the Heart Sutra) states: "Form is empty, and emptiness is form; emptiness thus is not different from form, nor is form different from emptiness."

The Northern school of Chan (Zen) furthered the Mahayana theory of the Six Paramitas, as seen in the following quotes:

To get rid of the eye thief, depart from the realm of form by having no grudge in the mind, this is what is called *dana* giving. To stop the ear thief, to wipe off the dust of sound, not to admit any form of idleness, this is *sila*, keeping the rules. To expel the nose thief, and to make all good and bad smells equal, this is called *ksanti* patience with insult. To control the tongue thief, not admit lewd taste, to chant and teach only Buddhist sutras, this is *virya* zeal in practice. Block the body thief, and confronted with poisonous thirst and desires, keep the mind still and unmoved, this is what is called *dhyana* Chan. To stop the mind thief, not to follow the dark unillumined, always perfect enlightened intuition, delighting in deeds of merit, this is *prajna* wisdom. If one is always able to stop the six thieves, to continuously purify the six roots, this is called to practice the Six Paramitas (crossings).[12]

The Northern school of Chan did its best to destroy the false notion that things were real (*fazhi*, attachment to things as if they were real). They did this by teaching that the Tathagata Storehouse (Rulai Dhzang) was not to be taken as a real entity. They realized that by destroying illusions, the practioners would meet with true mind, but feared that mind itself might then be taken as a reality. In teaching that one should become a Buddha, they feared that the practitioner would take the Buddha to be real. Thus, what was established had to be eradicated, and what was built up had to be torn down.

    Q. What about the Way of "Thinking without name" (Wuming Xiangfa)?

    A. That which the mind seeks within is to prove that world and self do not exist. To explain this, it says that name is false, which is the same as saying that *xiang* phenomena are false. To see, hear, know, and feel, which if these has name or differentiating form?

    Q. What can one do to ascend to the realm of no form?

> A. The person so doing does not know the true method. All such systems simply put mind to rest. If one seeks to calm the mind by force, the effort will be lost. The Sutra says: "Monks, it is like a dog running to bite a stone, not knowing that the stone was thrown by a man. Instead of biting the stone, let the dog bite the man. If he bit the man, then the mind would be at rest. For those who seek the Way, when the mind is emptied one returns to the (state of a) Buddha (Tathagata).

The kind of Chan taught here instructs the aspirant not to seek for the mind by extinguishing delusive thoughts. Instead it teaches that from the ontological viewpoint, the mind is not originally false. Such a viewpoint goes beyond Dao Xin (580-651, the fourth Chan patriarch) and Hong Ren's doctrine of nurturing a clear and calm mind by remaining tranquil. It further teaches that both action and tranquillity are forms of Chan meditation. Chan meditation can be practiced when moving as well as when quietly sitting. From this time on the great doorways to Sung Neo-confucianism, to "keeping the one," and the emphasis on respect were opened.

The Northern school of Chan made a clear distinction between those who preached the doctrine of liberation (the Buddhist) and those to whom the doctrine was passed on.

> Q. If one can only become a Buddha after saving all sentient beings, then how is it that a Buddha exists before all beings are saved?
>
> A. The Buddha himself has explained it: it is like a host who fans the flames in order to enlighten his guests. But while blowing on the flames, the host himself is first enlightened. The Bodhisattva means to aid all sentient beings crossover to enlightenment. But since his merit is complete, he first becomes a Buddha before all others.

The Northern school of Chan teaches the Dhyana technique of not seeking the Dao outside the self, but to turn inward to find it. Once realizing that the mind in its original nature is the Buddha, then one can instantly attain total liberation.

> If a seeker does not follow this way
> His/her efforts are spent in vain.
> The wise person seeks the mind, not the Buddha; when the mind is understood, nothing remains to be known.

From the time of Bodhidharma onward, the Chan (Zen) school did not rely on the written word, but spoke of profound principles directly, in a face-to-face encounter between master and disciple. One part of the method of teaching was based on principle, the other on actual practice. During the time of practice, the master had to teach the disciple how to "keep the one" point of meditative concentration, and how to quiet the heart by his own example and physical demonstration. Such methods could not rely on the written word. In the course of the presentation, the master had to offer explanations in many different ways, enlightening each student according to their capacity for understanding. Many Chan masters came from peasant families, while some were in fact illiterate, or were not good at expressing themselves through the written word. This is perhaps a more objective explanation of the fact that the Chan masters did not depend on the written word. Even though the Chan masters may not have been highly cultured, their powers of wisdom were extraordinary. Before enlightenment of humble origins, after awakening they could jump over the ten stages of perfection in a single bound. Here again we see one of the greatest differences between Chan and the other schools of Buddhism.

For a lengthy period of time academicians have mistakenly held that there was a great discrepancy between the northern and southern schools of Chan. It was thought that the southern school put greater emphasis on the spoken word leading to sudden enlightenment, while the northern school stressed gradual enlightenment after much practice. The southern school emphasized insightful wisdom while the northern school practiced sitting meditation. This is most probably a mistaken interpretation. The Chan methods of the northern school did use the method of interpreting spoken sayings (koan) and sudden enlightenment. Some of their most recondite beliefs were in fact no different from those of the southern school. If no explanation were given, perhaps it would not be recognized that many passages were inserted into the Platform Sutra which did not come from Hui Neng's school.

If one examines the extant materials of Shen Xiu's school, it would be evident that Shen Xiu and Hui Neng belonged to the same school. In fact, it would appear that there were two branches of the same school. Texts that resemble each other are more numerous than those which differ. If we approach the problem from its source, we can say that the tendency of the southern school was to favor sudden enlightenment, while the stress of the northern school was on gradual practice. But this distinction was a later development. During the time of Shen Xiu and Hui Neng, both schools practiced sudden enlightenment through gradual practice. Gradual practice was a technique for sudden enlightenment. Once enlightened, there were still many things that brought about attachments, requiring a continual awakening of the self in order that the fruits of enlightenment be solidified. There were indeed differences between the two schools, but these differences were not, as the texts of Hui Neng's followers proposed, a great problem of deviation from the true meaning of Chan. If we compare the differences between Hui Neng and Shen Xiu to the much more profound dissimilarities between Chan and the Tiantai, Huayan and Faxiang schools, the differences between the two Chan schools seem minor indeed. The differences between the southern and northern schools are real, but not very great.

The preface to the Dunhuang manuscript copy of the *Guan Xin Lun*, written by an anonymous monk, has the following:
> Dao is in the mind. *Li* principle has no fixed rule. *Bhutathata* thusness is obscure and hidden, beyond the gateway of healing. One cannot use words to plumb its depths. Do not establish the mind, then there will be nothing on which to impress the seal of dharma. Caught in name and form, one is lost in the Three Worlds' (past, present, and future) wheel of life and death. Absorbed in quiet, sunk in the void, the Buddha nature of itself is buried. Wisdom's non-being is beyond the causation of all existence. Use the marvel of non-being to transcend the realm of the void. To allow the mind to be involved in phenomena, makes a false sage, who cannot escape the wheel of life and death (samsara). By deliberately seeking to void the mind and grasp the void, one becomes maddened by everyday life and buried in the sea of suffering. This is why the monk Bodhidharma grieved for those deluded in crossing, and taught how to break all phenomenal images... by giving up neither being or non-being, letting the two *satya* forms of knowing (ordinary and enlightened) exist side-by-side.[13]

This text, attributed in a gloss to a monk named *Po Xiang Lun* Bodhidharma, is not the same as the *Prajna Sunya* (Empty Wisdom) school that promotes the sweeping away of all forms of thought. It teaches the enlightening the original (unsullied) mind in order to escape forever the wheel of life-and-death, not unlike the "Four practices for entering the Way" (Ru Dao Sixing) of the early Chan (Zen) schools. Such practices are in accord with the teachings of Shen Xiu's northern school of Chan.

The *Guan Xin Lun* teaches that there are two kinds of mind, the pure and the impure. Both exist simultaneously. The student of Chan is supposed to foster the pure mind, and reduce the impure. A pure mind is the basis for entering Buddhahood, while the contaminated mind has no original substance. By dispelling the three poisons (concupiscence, anger, ignorance), one can attain to a quiet mind, without the seeds (of thought) sprouting. All acts of perfecting or contemplation are done to increase the pure mind and eradicate the sullied mind. It was the later followers of the school who emphasized the contemplation of mind, perfecting of stillness and cleansing from impurity, by not leaving the path of gradual enlightenment.

But the contemplation of mind, the perfecting of deeds, cannot be separated from the mind. "In order to attain the Pure Buddha Land, one must purify the heart. When the mind is pure, then the Buddha land is pure." This is the same as saying that the purity and impurity of the world is only in the mind. The Pure Land is inside, not outside man. Because of this, they were against chanting the name of Buddha. The *Guan Xin Lun* says:

> Those who chant the Buddha's name must do so correctly.
> To eliminate thoughts is correct; not to do so is wrong.
> For *nien* chant is a calling to mind or memory.
> *Nien* visualized chant belongs to the mind, not words.
> That which comes from the mouth is called *sung* chant;
> That which is in the mind is called *nian* to visualize.
> Therefore to know that visualization is from the mind,
> is to name the gateway to awakening. Chants only from the mouth, are sounds coming from phenomenal illusion.

The *nian* visualized chant of Chan is done in order to keep the Buddha continually in mind, a way of strengthening the practice of transforming the mental process. It is not found in the vocal chanting of the Buddha's name. It follows therefore that all forms of differentiation come from within the mind, and that all sorts of external practices aside from cleansing the mind are unnecessary. Here indeed we find the doorway opening to the liberal practices of later Chan Buddhism.

Owing to its close association with the powers of the central government, northern Chan received strong political support from emperors and high ranking officials.[14] One of its obvious advantages was its home base on Song Shan near Loyang, in Henan Province. Due to its proximity to the eastern capital of Loyang, the school was able to develop undisturbed over a lengthy period of time. After the rebellion of the two generals An Lu Shan and Shi Siming (752 AD), the central government was faced with numerous crises, and continuous internal warfare. Northern Chan, however, was able to sustain its base for nearly another hundred years, i.e., until the Fifth Year of the Hui Chang reign (815) when when Emperor Wu began the abolition of Buddhism. Along with other Buddhist schools, Northern Chan suffered a disastrous blow, and was never restored to its previous prosperity. Based on records taken from the *Jingde Chuan Deng Lu* (Records of the Transmission of the Lamp from the Jingde period, 1004-1107), *Jin shih cui bian* (A Collection of Bronze and Stone Inscriptions), and the *Song Gaoseng Zhuan* (Biographies of Eminent Monks of the Song Dynasty, 988 AD), and other stone and bronze records, we find that many monks of the Northern Chan school were indeed of great renown (during the Tang period). E.g., the monk Fa Ru had a disciple called Li Yuansui (644-716), Shen Xiu taught Jing Xian (660-723), who in turn taught Fa Xuan, Hui Xian, Jing Yan and Hui Ling. There were also other disciples, such as Hui Kong (?-773), Ling Zhu (690-746), Si Gong (701-784), Ling Yun (?-729), Jing Shun (?-750), and 25 other disciples of Pu Ji (651-739).

Yi Fu and the monk Yixing learned Tantric practices from Vajrabodhi, while such noted masters as Zhen Gong (739-829), Cong Yan (753-837), Heng Zheng (? - 843), Ri Zhao, Huan Pu, Qing Zhu (806-888), Dao Shu (733-825), Chen Guan (760-820), Fa Wan (715-790) were all in the line of monks who were in the transmission lineage of the Northern Chan master Pu Ji.

As mentioned above, Shen Xiu's school of Northern Chan enjoyed a long period of patronage by the court and the aristocrats of the central Tang government. Since forms of Tantric Buddhism were popular during the reign of the Emperor Xuan

Zong, many of the Chan (Zen) masters studied Tantric Buddhism as well as Dhyana (Chan). Pu Ji's disciple Yi Fu received a Tantric transmission from Vajrabodhi, while Bao Wei and Ming Wei received an Abhiseka from Subhakarasimha. The Great Tantric Master Hui Guo (753-805) also passed on Tantric Buddhism, and was aided in translating the Tantric scriptures by Wen Zo, a disciple of Shen Xiu. Another disciple of Shen Xiu named Jing Xian received an *abhiseka* ordination from Subhakarasimha.

The fact that monks of the medieval period sought support from the imperial court and its officials is reflected in the practices of the times. It was a medieval court custom that emperors and high ranking officials be honored with posthumous titles. Empress Wu of the Tong dynasty directed that Shen Xiu be given the posthumous title Da Tong Chan Master. Yi Fu was entitled Da Zhui Chan Master, and Pu Ji was named Da Zhao Chan Master. Such titles prove the close ties of the Chan monks with the government.

At a later period the Southern Chan masters were also honored with posthumous titles. Hui Neng was entitled Da Jian Chan Master, Xing Si was Hong Ji Chan Master, Dao Yi was named Da Ji Chan master. All of these titles were confirmed some 100 years after the death of the master. This comparison reflects the less favored position of the Southern Chan school at the beginning of its history. After the death of Shen Xiu and Yi Fu, the Northern and Southern schools waged an increasingly intense struggle in contending for the position of orthodox transmission of the Dharma, and the arrangement of transmission lineages. In the *Song Yue Si Pei* (stone inscription of Mt. Song Monastery) Li Yong records:

> Bodhidharma Bodhisattva transmitted his teachings to Hui Ke. Hui Ke gave it to Seng Can, Seng Can to Dao Xin, Dao Xin to Hong Ren, Hong Ren to Shen Xiu. Shen Xiu's disciple is the present monk Pu Yi.

The tablet was erected in 739 when Pu Ji was still alive. He was acknowledged at that time to be the inheritor of the direct line of transmitted teachings from the patriarch.

The Song Shan-Luoyang area was the home base of the Northern School of Chan for a lengthy period time, during which the Southern school actually spread its influence into North China. An example of this is the Chan Master Tian Ran from Dan Xia, Zhejiang Province (738-824).[15] came from the south to Loyang to spread his doctrines. The Biography of Famous Monks (up to the) Song Period reports that "the whole region of Loyang naturally followed him as their teacher. Wei Kuan and Xiu Jing later came to Loyang to give instructions (in southern Chan).[16] The Northern School, on the other hand, did not spread to south China. These documents show the spread of the Southern School, gradually leading to a position of dominance throughout China.

We have mentioned above that the southern and northern schools eventually became irreconcilable enemies. This study suggests that in fact their doctrines were not that much different from each other. Neither were the differences the result of academic debate. In fact from the extant materials that remain from the two schools, their methods of practice, theoretical teachings, and modes of thought were quite close. The radical position of breaking from words and images and completely eradicating all concepts are found in the Platform Sutra as well as in Shen Xiu's writings. Both Shen Xiu and Hui Neng stressed that one should neither be attached to nor give up reading the sutras, neither basing everything on sitting meditation, or giving it up entirely. The conservative image of Shen Xiu's school was created by the later followers of Hui Neng's school. Shen Xiu was in fact a very liberal thinker. The strife between the Southern and Northern school was not so much an academic debate as a struggle for political power.

THE MULTI-ETHNIC CHARACTER
OF CHINESE BUDDHISM

by Du Jiwen

When speaking of traditional Chinese culture, Buddhism is always given a very important place. Born in India, nourished in Central Asia, Buddhism may first have entered China at the end of the Western Han period.[1] When seen from the Chinese Cultural viewpoint, Buddhism is called a foreign religion, something which is not quite *zheng* orthodox in the traditional Chinese sense. Thus from the time when Buddhism's "horns and hooves" first appeared in Chinese society, it was the object of much persecution and prejudicial discrimination. From the end of the Han through the Wei dynasties (ca. 200-260 CE) when the *Sanjiao* "Three Religions" controversy became dominant, until the northern and southern Sung dynasties (960-1281 CE) when Taoist masters were influential, Buddhism suffered a total of four major suppressions and innumerable lesser persecutions. The results of all these attempts at curtailment are well known. Buddhism was not suppressed or quieted. Transmitted continuously over the past 2,000 years, it eventually became an integral part of Chinese culture. Not only did the descendants of the saffron robed monks bring about a marvelous unity between foreign and Chinese culture, but they added a quiet dignity to the very nature of Chinese society, which influenced neighboring cultures to the East and South.

Such a phenomenon needs an adequate explanation, and in fact there are many reasons advanced to explain it. One of the most popular is that Buddhism became "Chinese," i.e., China eventually changed Buddhism, adapting and unifying it with its own cultural system.

I agree with this position, and feel that it is a realistic assessment. Yet what must be emphasized here is that the influence was not one sided, i.e., not as Mencius would have said, "China influences the *Yi* barbarians," but rather that China itself was influenced by non-Han peoples. Our research up to the present has not laid sufficient emphasis on this latter aspect, i.e., the influence of the non-Han on the Chinese.

Historically speaking, Buddhism is the first culture from outside to deeply challenge and effect traditional hardbound culture found within China. Its entrance and spread profoundly effected the very core of China's social, economic, cultural, and intellectual system, in a way that people of today would find difficult to imagine. Buddhism has a very special system of thought and attitude towards the world. Once accepted, it radically changed the cultural structure of the Qin-Han model, and gave rise to a system or Way of even more profound significance. When examined from this (social as well as cultural) aspect, it was not only Chinese monks who spread its teachings in China. Many Chinese living abroad and minority ethnic groups can be found who had a profound influence on the very marrow of the Confucian bones. One of the reasons for this phenomenon, i.e., that Buddhism could absorb many external cultural norms and unify these elements within Chinese culture, was precisely because it was not only formulated by ethnic Chinese, but included in its most influential members Chinese who had lived abroad and non-Han ethnic minorities. When we take note of the multi-ethnic composition of Chinese Buddhism, we see that one of the unexpected shortcomings in its study up to now has been the insufficient notice given to this fact.

From the Wei-Qin period until the Five Dynasties and the beginning of the Sung (220-960 CE), i.e., nearly 1,000 years, Buddhism was a most lively and vibrant element in China's feudal culture. One of the causes of its fertility, indeed the reason why it could penetrate Chinese society and pierce to the very marrow of the Confucian bones, was because it could unfailingly breath in elements from outside, passed through many ethnic hands, to enrich the inner self. Repeatedly we see it recover from deep wounds, arise refreshed, to establish new schools, each with its own special characteristics. If it did not have these special qualities, it could not have survived. After the northern and southern Sung dynasties (960-1281 CE), Buddhism bogged down. The various schools were amalgamated. Standard Buddhist scholarship almost always loses sight of the special historical characteristics of each of the schools, and from this they lost sight of the special function in creating a place in cultural thought. This is another shortcoming in Buddhist research.

These few points mentioned above, are a questions that I have had in studying the history of Buddhism. I would be most gratified if the reader would help me in resolving these problems, as a sort of dialogue that might prove useful to a deeper understanding of Chinese Buddhism.

I

The First Emperor of the Qin Dynasty (221-206 BCE) used legalist methods to unify China. This was changed at the beginning of the Western Han period (206 BC - 1 CE) first to *Huanglau* Daoism, then to the sole usage of *Ru* Confucianism from the reign of the Han Emperor Wu (140-86 BCE). That the theoretical basis for unifying China could change so frequently in less than 100 years, and on such a wide scale, can only be explained by the feudal nature of society. By the same token, such a purely theoretical basis for unifying a nation could not last for a long period of time. By the end of the Eastern Han (25-220 CE) the Yin-Yang Five Element prognostication system which was the structural basis at the core of the Confucian political system, had come to the end of its tenure. We can see that the Imperial Court had lost faith in it, for the Huan Emperor (147-167 CE) had already used Buddhist and Taoist rites in imperial court ritual, a sure sign of change. The peasants, on the other hand, in accepting the *chan* rites of (village) repentance, had in fact cast aside the

Five Classics, and accepted the teachings of the *Taiping Jingling* scripture, (*The Pure Guide to Great Peace*) of Zhang Jiao, leader of the Yellow Turbans (in East China). The (Taoist) Zhang Lu used the Laozi to rule Hanzhong (Sichuan-Shaanxi, West China), while Cao Cao used Punitive laws to organize the government (of N. China). At the same time that the *qingyi* "Pure Discussion" intellectual movement was at its height, the gentry officials (shidafu) most frequently favored Taoist philosophy, and furthermore followed the tendency of collecting books that recorded extraordinary wonders and marvels.

It was within this cultural and intellectual background that Buddhism began a period of great development and expansion. Furthermore, it was due to the same gentry officials and to Chinese monks who had traveled abroad, that this expansion was first able to take place.

What we have called "gentry officials" in this study were in fact all intellectuals of the landlord class. This level of feudal society could not have been other than intellectual reactionaries whose power would oppose change in society. By the same token they were also an important barometer of social change and power redistribution within that society. They had experienced two great upheavals at the end of the Han period (The popular Taiping Yellow Turban revolt and the rebellion of the Eunuchs at court) and their spirits were at a low ebb. The fires and devastation that laid waste to society at the end of the Han left them with no choice but to seek a new weltanschauung, a new path and meaning to life. The period that lasted from the end of Emperor Huan's reign, that brought an end to the Han, to the end of the Wei-Jin period (186-420 CE) was one of great difficulty and hardship. It was a time of agitation, and searching for guidelines.

It was precisely at this time, i.e., an age and a half of indecisiveness, that Buddhism in its most authentic form was discovered. Its profound philosophy of human life and its strange new religious vision deeply moved the heart strings of the intellectual gentry, evoking a vibrant movement that shook the very earth. If the human world was originally what Buddhism said it was, if all sorrows and troubles could indeed be cast aside, then the sullied world can by this very fact become pure and peaceful. The people could create a new direction to life diametrically opposite to traditional Chinese culture. This innovative way of thinking, along with the formulation of many kinds of new thought systems, began with the movement to teach Buddhist doctrines and translate scriptures as represented by the work of An Shi Gao (148-186 CE) and Zhilou Jiachen (147-264 CE).

An Shi Gao was a Parthian, while Zhilou Jiachen was an Indo-Scythian. The Parthians, who flourished between 100 BCE and 300 CE, extended the Kingdom of Parthia from the Mediterranean Sea in the West all the way to the northeast of India. The Indo-Scythians, who began their expansion from 200 BCE, began to spread from the Amur river southwestward, reaching the upper reaches of the Indus River within a century, and founding a Buddhist kingdom known in Chinese history as the Kingdom of Kusana. These two great nations, besides establishing cultural relations with the ancient kingdoms of Greece, Persia, India, and China, could not but leave a fresh indelible imprint on Buddhism.

The carving of Buddhist statues was directly based on the artistic models of Greece and Ghandara (present day Pakistan), an influence that is commonly recognized today. The earlier Buddhist scriptures translated into Chinese show the definite influence of Greek Philosophy. After the influence of Persian Zoroastrianism on Buddhism, and the coming of Zoroastrianism and Manichees to China, these movements were had a greatly effected Buddhism, a further proof of our hypothesis. This is especially true of the texts of Tantric Buddhism, particularly those sections of the Canon called $Zami^2$ (miscellaneous Tantric texts), which latter show a different origin from original Buddhist roots. The Chinese versions of these texts occur perhaps more than a hundred years earlier than the Indian (Siddham sanskrit) versions, clearly suggesting that they were in fact formulated in Central Asia. Seen from the structural viewpoint, they seem to fall under the category of local (central Asian) primitive religion. Because of these facts, the Buddhism from these areas that came into China brought with it many of the elements of the various peoples to the west, influencing Chinese society and culture in a variety of different ways.

According to hagiographical references, An Shi Gao was a Parthian Prince who became a monk for political reasons. He journeyed to Luoyang at the beginning of Emperor Huan's reign years (184 CE), then traveled to the area south of the Yangzi river during the disturbances at the end of the Ling Emperor's reign (189 CE). He traveled as far south as Guangzhou, and died at Kuaiji. He was active in China for more than forty years, spreading for the most part the Theravada-Nikaya[3] doctrines. It is believed that China's earliest translated text, the *Sutra in Forty-two Chapters* and its doctrines were popular at this time. The religious ideas being discussed included the value, origin, and freeing of self from the conditions of human life. The doctrines that the human condition was not permanent, that the human body "had no atman" (i.e., no self origination), and that human life was basically conditioned by suffering, touched the surface of the entire scholar gentry class, and moved some very deeply.

We must pay close attention to the fact that the person who accepted these ideas was snatched away from the moral-ethical political system of family and nation, and given a wholly new and independent way of viewing reality, a method quite the opposite of traditional Chinese thinking. Buddhism looked on the family as a sort of imprisoning cage, and all acts proper to human nature, including marriage, as sources of human suffering. It was even more opposed to logical discourse and court politics. Because of this it advocated shaving the head, celibacy, poverty, and cutting off all connections with family and society, in order to attain a life of peace and quiet away from the world. This sort of spiritual ideal China had never seen before, even from the most ancient of times. It was a complete and total reversal of a religious and ritual system based on blood ties and their relationships, as well as the corresponding world view and value system that included the "Three duties and five constants," (the entire Confucian ethical system, i.e., duties to prince, father, and husband; filiality, reciprocity, benevolence, loyalty, respect, ed. note), other familial and friendship ties, and so forth.

Of the many schools of Theravada-Nikaya Buddhism, that with the longest and most influential history is the Realist School or Mulasarvastivadah.[4] It was this school that An Shi Gao first spread in China. The theoreticians of the school were especially prolific, right up until the time that Xuanzang (596-664 CE) introduced his translations (of the Yogacara idealist teachings) ca. 648 CE. Those who supported and followed this school's world view and ascetical theories, the so called *sarvabhava* (all exists)[5] school, held sway and dominated over a lengthy period of time. The Vaibhasikas (Sarvastivadins) and the Abhidharmakosa (of Paramartha, ca. 556 CE) also followed the doctrines and practical teachings of the Realist School. The philosophy of the Realists not only dominated the theoretical discussions of the clergy-monks of the two Jin and the North-South Kingdoms, but also influenced worldly scholars and literati as well. According to the point of departure of the Realists discussions, one must re-examine the Vaipulya theory "On reverencing all existence," a theory especially clear in the writings attributed to a southern Song dynasty Arhat "On Rebirth."[6]

However, if one investigates the origins of the Realist School, one must pursue the point as far back as ancient Greece. From Parmenides' theory of existence to Plato's idealism, one can find a number of similarities within Buddhist schools of thought. This is not only a theoretical comparison; there are indeed historical bases for the analogy. The center for Buddhist realism was Gandara and Kashmir, places where Greek influence was most heavily felt. The Greeks had built a great center there by 200 BCE. Its famous ruler King Melinda, who used military force to subdue the region along the adjacent rivers, was a patron of Buddhism. Two volumes in the Chinese Canon, the *Biksu Nagasena Sutras*[7] are extant, which describe the conversion of King Melinda to Buddhism. A special feature of these two books is that they do not use the standard format of explaining the Buddha's sayings, as do the sutras, or the Abhidamma-pitaka form of the (Pali Canon) philosophical treatises. Rather, they are written as a question and answer dialogue, in the style of logical discourse. The texts do not speak of the rules of the monk or of meditation, but rather treat of wisdom and the superior role of the wise man, reflecting the Greek spirit and manner. The texts have a Pali version; the extant Chinese text seems to be the oldest, the original version of which, according to some scholars, was in Greek. The thought patterns of the Nagasena Biksu Texts follows that of the Sarvastivada.[8]

Zhilou Jiachen's life and teachings are no longer transmitted. He came to Luoyang more or less at the end of the Huan Emperor's reign, ca. 167 CE. There is a record of the works he translated during the reign of Emperor Ling, 178-189 CE. The works he translated were all of the Mahayana tradition, the most important being from the Prajnaparamita Canon.

The Prajnaparamita texts provided a form of philosophical world view and *upaya* convenient or skillful means (of enlightenment), which in summary held that all things had a single origin. Together with Malasarvastivadah, it is one of the theoretical bases for early Chinese Buddhism. The others were the Wei-Jin periods (220-419 CE) Prajna wisdom, the so-called "Yao-qin old theory of the Guan-Ho region (northwest China),"[9] and the Sui-Tang Madhyamika school, both of which came under the Prajnaparamita system of thought. According to Prajna theory, the very substance of ordinary human knowledge is empty and false. All of the phenomenal objects of thought are relative, i.e., things produced through pure subjectivity. They do not represent any sort of truly objective reality. It therefore assumed an attitude of skepticism and doubt about all phenomena, and in the last resort denied the substantial reality of all things. This form of relatively total skepticism, although it was concentrated on opposing Buddhism's denial of traditional authority, still as a kind of philosophy concerned with the very principles of knowing, could not but form a serious threat to the traditional authority and position of Confucianism as well. The first manifestation of this (threat) was that it turned the scholar officials from the traditional patriarchal clan system, and had the cynical effrontery to supply a brand new form of logic, in doing so. The Prajna theories thus had a deeply influential drawing power on the scholar officials. (This can be seen by) the translation of the *Vimalikirti-Nirdesa*[10] sutra undertaken by the monk Zhi Qian, of Scythian descent, in the Sun-Wu area during the Three Kingdoms period. This text elaborated the Prajna theories of adaptability, and lack of conventional restraint. The scholar officials were bowled over by it. The Tang poet Wang Wei (701-761 CE) went so far as to take the title "Malakirti"[11] as a pen name. Buddhism thus used Prajna thought as a means of access to the upper classes from its earliest period. Step-by-sep Prajna thought was transformed into an important element of Neo-Taoist *Xuanxue* thinking as well.

Concerning belief in the Pure Land, during the Cao-Wei period (220-264 CE), the monk Sanghavarman translated the *Sukha-vativyuha Sutra*[12] (ca. 252 CE, at White Horse monastery, in Luoyang, ed. note). Its influence reached everywhere. The text spoke of a kingdom that was without poverty, hunger, cold, or war, without division, pain, or sorrow, where all humans were one family, a world that was a paradise. Concerning the ideal of a heavenly paradise, it was seen as a crossing over from the oppressive evil (of the present world) to a land that was inconceivable to the Confucian state of great unity, or the Taoist refuge for the downtrodden. The Buddhist vision of crossing over to the other shore, which was seen as a counterpart to this world of oppressive suffering, and the imprint left by formulating this kind of belief, found a market and was spread first and foremost among the scholar official class. Only then did it enter into the belief of the common folk and the court. Its influence was broad and long lasting.

The "Way of the Bodhisattva" took the salvation of all sentient beings as its basic doctrine, and the "six crossings" as its internal content. The way of saving all sentient beings was the direct opposite of the Theravada doctrine of the Arhat (individual striving for perfection). It was also contrary to the traditional Chinese notion of the centrality of the Chinese family and nation. The term "six crossings" was used in reference to actually saving all sentient beings, one of the strongest factors in giving it access to and making it a part of the daily life of the masses. During the Sun-Wu period (222-277 CE) the Sogdian monk Sanghavarman (from present day Samarkand) translated the *Collected Sutras of the Six Paramitas*,[13] mentioning the Buddhist emphasis on the doctrine of universal salvation. He used the Buddhist doctrines to lay out a powerful plan to convince the rulers to promote a benevolent government, a society without war, robbery, or prisons, a paradise on earth where every human being had an abundance of things to wear and eat. He was the first person after the death of Mencius some 500 years earlier to promote Mencius' doctrines on the good of the people, laying heavy emphasis on the need to judge the prince's virtue from the well being of the people, and the power pf the people to grant authority to the ruler. But what can guarantee good relations between the people and the ruler? Not Confucian theories of virtue but rather the Buddhist notion of cause and effect in rewarding or punishing human acts, the five rules of conduct and the ten good deeds. This sort of thinking that emphasized the good of all sentient beings, ideas quite far from the then ruling authorities, was the main current of early Chinese Buddhist teaching.

Sanghavarman and Sanghapala were Sogdian monks. Sogdia (Samarkand) was a kingdom to the east of Parthia and to the north of Indo-Scythia, between the Aral Sea and Lake Balkhash. There were many Han people living there who traveled to and from China. Sanghavarma's ancestors were from India. His father had engaged in trade and lived in many places. Thus in later years he became with Zhi Qian one of the founders of Buddhism in the southern Sun-Wu Kingdom.

Historians have debated the remarkable influence that early Buddhism had on the people of China. The *Hou Han Ji*[14] records of Buddhism that: "What it seeks is within the body, and what it explains are things that can be seen and heard. Yet it is mysterious and deep, and difficult to fathom." The *Hou Han Shu* says of it: "It speaks of things great beyond experience, wonders and oddities it has not fathomed. Zou Yen (Yin-Yang Five Element Theory) treats of nature's changes, and Zhuangzi discusses snail horns. Yet Buddhism has not come close to explaining anything."[15] Both of these authors say the same thing. Buddhist formal logic was quite different from traditional Chinese inductive empiricism (experience based thinking). Its abstract form of analysis and religious vision transcended experience, and made scholars of traditional Chinese learning alarmed beyond measure.

The basis of Chinese philosophy during the Qin-Han period was a form of concrete or inductive empiricism. It reached its zenith in the skeptical empiricist writings of Wang Chung. The Northern dynasty (420-583 CE) scholar Yen Zhitui wrote: "All that man believes in comes from the ears and eyes,"[16] which is indeed the point of departure of all *Ru* Confucian philosophy. Zhuangzi's explanation: "Outside of the six joinings (n.b., east, south, west, north, center, up, down, space-time experience), the sage contemplates but does not discuss,"[17] is also based on inductive empiricism. Buddhism thus took a firm stand against empiricism as its starting point.

Both Zhi Dun (Zhi Daolin, 314-366 CE) and Hui Yuan (ca. 402 CE) held that all of China's perennial thinkers and sages could not but rely on knowledge that was limited to or derived from personal experience, (body, eyes, ears), so that things that hadn't been discussed or heard before, or trod on by the soles of their own shoes, they judged to be non-existent. But Buddhism, on the contrary, was concerned with discussing things quite beyond ordinary experience. Therefore they used abstract logic and deductive analysis which consistently transcended the level of trivial debate. When meeting with the abstract and arbitrary style of the New-Taoist thinkers, Buddhism greatly influenced them to adopt a terse and comprehensive style of debate. Buddhism from its very beginning was able to assume a dominant intellectual position because it discussed such things as human origins, unequal social roots, the substance of the universe, the structure of things, ideas hitherto quite rare in China's intellectual history. It was only after the coming and spread of Buddhism in China that this profound level of philosophical discourse entered into the deepest layers of Chinese thought.

Of the abundant religious images introduced by Buddhism, that which most deeply affected the noble and intellectual classes, that which they most feared losing for their own good, and which led to most self doubt was the theory of co-dependent origination, i.e., cause and effect, life and death, blessing and failure as a result of human deeds, good or bad

"Cause and effect, retribution for deeds," was a theory that was most widespread and had the deepest effect among the ordinary people and the middle classes. It must be given first and most important place amongst all religious concepts in China. From the Song period (960 CE) until today in drama, song, fiction, and novels, the works of China's literary giants all used this concept as a guiding compass of Buddhist thought, even to the extent of degrading it to the role of oppressing human livelihood. Furthermore, this sort of widely accepted concept actually supported a value deeply embedded in the cultural soil of China. The religious system that came as part and parcel of the West and East Han periods believed in the ancestral system and a Heavenly Emperor. Prognostic techniques and shaman-medium practices were an adjunct to it. All of these elements put together supported the system of ancestral lineage and imperial rule. Although there was already cognate the idea of a "cause and effect" response to good and bad deeds, the people who were actually responsible to the "Dao (Way) of Heaven" i.e., who received Heaven's reward and punishment, were the clans and rulers.

Buddhism's response to this was to reverse the theory of Heaven's Will as being the sole responsibility of clans and kings. Instead it proposed the theory that each individual's deeds were responsible, i.e., the cause for blessing or punishment (N.b., Karma means deeds). It therefore pointed out that words and deeds were willed, and that reward and punishment were in fact meted out according to each person's willed actions. In other words, each person created his or her own surroundings and circumstances, good or bad luck. There was no real causal relationship with external forces other than one's deeds. This sort of system, with its mystic trappings, was diametrically opposed to the basics of the deep-rooted family system, and declared a sort of war on the nation's political system. From the above we can judge the earth-shaking effect that Buddhism had (on China).

Buddhism from abroad and its human values, political theory, religious philosophy, collided head-on with traditional Chinese culture. All through the ages those who opposed Buddhism accused it of having no father, no ruler, and no heaven, and thus of destroying the nation, family, and the human body. Though such a serious level of opposition should have had serious consequences, in fact many scholars chose to justify Buddhist beliefs. The first Chinese author to come to the defense of Buddhism was Mouzi, whose work *Mouzi Li Huo Lun*[18] (Mouzi's clarification of doubt about Buddhism) was written sometime between the late han and the Wei period (220-260 CE). In this work he proposed: "Abandon the Confucian heroes (Shun, Zhou Gong, Confucius), learn from the barbarians (Yi and Di minorities), and "The Land of the Han (China) is not the center of the world," and "Books need not only carry the sayings of Confucius." He further taught that "The *Junzi* man of noble character should utilize all sorts of beneficial practices to perfect the physical body."[19]

These texts show clearly that a portion of the scholar official class had from an early period accepted Buddhist teachings to oppose traditional principles of leadership and belief. The use of Buddhist teachings among the higher levels of learned Confucian and Taoist scholars,[20] giving a special Buddhist direction to intellectual discourse. Buddhist scolars had to continually provide intellectual weapons in response to those who chose to oppose the authority of tradition, a phenomenon that has been true through the Ming and Qing Dynasties right up to the present.

Concurrent with the earliest Buddhist movement and its criticism came changes in Daoism and the Fangshu liturgists and healers of the Qin-Han period, i.e., a movement towards an organized Taoist religion. From this was forged a new sort of intellectual system hitherto unseen in the structure of feudal thought, i.e., Confucianism, Daoism, and Buddhism became like three legs of a tripod. The three religious teachings were thus established and regulated as a single (religious-cultural) *ding* (alchemical or liturgical "vessel") which brought about a period of struggle and adjustment not settled until the Sui-Tang period (581-906 CE), when the collaborative aspect and function (work) of the three religions was more clearly delineated. The Tang Dynasty monk Zong Yan stated: "Confucianism for social ethics (zhong-xiao, social and family values), Daoism for the physical body, Buddhist compassion for all creatures." "A tripod has three legs, using them equally is its perfection; the three religious teachings must be equally respected; only thus can blessing be attained."[21] The Xiao Zong Emperor of the Song dynasty (1163-1190 CE) had the

Yuan Dao Lun (On the Primordial Tao) published, which stated: "Use Buddhism to perfect the heart, Taoism to nourish the body, and Confucianism to govern the world. Only then will all things go well." The theory of "Equally following the Three Religions" had the widest differing set of interpretations among the officials, monks, people, and court, yet the Three Religions could not but form a single cultural system, from beginning to end the keynote for social discourse. It must be admitted that this was one of the greatest events in the history of Chinese thought, that which delineated historical periods, the end of an epoch when Confucianism reigned supreme. Feudal thought formed a new structural pattern not experienced before. The appearance of this new structural pattern provided a whole new set of ideals for new life in society and cultural thought, and increased the ability to create new ways of human reasoning.

II

The Wei-Jin to the North-South dynasties (220-581 CE) when Buddhism as a foreign religion first flooded into the interior of China, was a period of rapid expansion . Not only did foreign monks come from India, Parthia, Tokharia, and Sogdiana (Samarkand), some even came from such far away places as Sri Lanka and the ancient kingdoms of Southeast Asia. Zhu Shixing and Faxian are examples of Chinese monks who retraced the steps of their spiritual ancestors westward to seek the Dharma, beginning a movement to seek the origins the new doctrines. Furthermore, if one looks at the causes that promoted the expansion of Buddhism, one could say that the period between the two Jin, i.e., between the North-South Dynasties and the (earlier) Han-Wei marked the boundary of two quite different eras. The point of departure for the birth of Buddhism during the Han-Wei were the stimuli of social-political and intellectual-cultural crises, while the spread of Buddhism during the later Qin-North South period was due mainly to relationships with people of multiethnic origin (i.e., Chinese and non-Han), and especially the support of Buddhism provided by the five (non-Chinese) Hun rulers of the northern dynasties.

Three areas in Chinese Turkestan, present day Xinjiang province, Khotan, Kucha and Kashgar were important communication routes along the Silk Road, places where Buddhism coming eastward and Chinese culture going westward converged. From the Wei-Jin period onward the comings and goings between this region and the interior of China flourished and increased day-by-day, an important element in the sinicization of Buddhism. The Prajnaparamita sutra flourished from a very early time in Khotan, which we know from the fact that the monk Zhu Shixing came here ca. 260 CE seeking Mahayana texts. The Khotanese-Kustana monk Moksala came to China during the Wei-Jin period, where he took part in translating the *Fang Guang Prajna* Sutra (Prajna Sutra for releasing lamps).[22] All of this is by way of showing that Khotan was an important supplier of Prajna materials and their study in China proper.

The famous monk Vasilimitra was of Kuchanese descent. His ancestors had moved to Qinyang in Henan. After becoming a monk he went to live in the Jianjing monastery in Changan, where his disciples numbered over 1000 monks. His fame spread from the Guan region (Changan) as far west as Dunhuang. In the Qin kingdom to the east of Xao Han (a pass on the Henan border) he was considered to be a holy sage. The Qin scholar San Chao in his *Treatise on Taoist Sages*[23] compared him with Xi Kang, one of the Seven Sages of the Bamboo Groves. Vasilimitra crossed to the land south of the Yangzi river towards the end of the Western Qin period (313 CE), where among his many other works now found in the Tantric section of the Buddhist Canon is the *Mayura Raja Mantra*.[24] He is believed to be the first tantric expert to live south of the Yangzi river. Vasilimitra was also quite good at *Xuantan* intellectual discourse, causing him to be ranked with

Wang Dao and other such intelligentsia. Wong Min praised him as follows: "Heaven has given us a great hero, why ask if he is Han or ethnic minority?"[25] Because of the special quality of excellence that the minority peoples brought to Buddhist teachings, they were able to enter quickly into the circles and social prominence of mainstream orthodox thinkers during the two Qin periods, (265-419 CE), and achieved equal cultural and intellectual status and fame (with Han thinkers). From this time onward a continuous flow of famous monks and scriptures came from Khotan and Kashgar.

Of all the famous Central Asian Hun and Han monks of the western Qin who had authority and influence over the common people, none surpassed that of Dharmaraksa (Zhu Fa Hu). Of Indo-Scythian descent, he lived in Dunhuang before becoming a monk. After (taking his Buddhist vows) he lived in Dunhuang, Jiuxian, and then Changan, where he translated sutras for 47 years. He brought with him much of the thought and feelings of the minority peoples of west China, and with it broke wide open the range of vision of the Han Chinese. His promotion of non-conceptual Prajna wisdom, as well as direct, intuitive, subjective apprehension and other such problems, made the greatest impact on Prajna thought of the Eastern Jin period (317-419 CE). Sun Chuo[26] said of Dharmaraksa "His virtue resides in the Realist school" (of Madhyamika), putting him on a par with Shan Dao of the Seven Sages of the Bamboo Groves. Special mention must be made of the many translations he did of texts that emphasized the importance of women, and of his high level of wisdom and ability to debate. His translations in this regard especially attacked those who looked down on women, particularly arguing against the prejudiced based on the superiority of the male sex. He taught that women could gain enlightenment equally with men, and that "in their next lives, they could become rulers." This sort of thinking is reflected in the two texts that he translated at the end of the Eastern Jin period, the *Da Yun Jing* and the *Sheng Man Jing*.[27]

Historically speaking, this tide of innovative thinking had a very profound effect on traditional Buddhist as well as Confucian thinking, in promoting the movement of equality of women in society and politics. Empress Hu's arrogation of power to herself during the Northern Wei and the Tang Empress Wu Ze Tian (684-704 CE) both were famous examples of women who had close connections with Buddhism. Even before Empress Wu, the lady Chen Shuozhen of Muzhou called herself *Wen Jia Huangdi* (Literary refined emperor). The separatist state she set up was an area which at the time was mostly populated with monks and faithful followers; the monks and masses led along by her were very many.

During the two Jin periods (W. Jin, 265-313; E. Jin, 317-419) the most important feature of those countries built by Han Chinese in which Buddhism spread was the number of noted monks who became famous scholars. The result of this, however, was that the famous monks did not because of their (literary qualities) lose the characteristics of their Buddhist roots. The renowned scholarly Sramanas (monks) forced the other schools, such as the Neo Taoist scholars who followed the "Three Principles for the Mystic," (Wang Bi, Guo Xiang, etc), the *Gui Wu* Taoists (who respected the Wu transcendent) and the *Chong You* realists, to follow the prevailing winds in order to keep their position. The Eastern Jin monk Zhi Dun wrote a commentary on the First Chapter of the Zhuangzi *Xiao Yao You*, adapting Zhuangzi scholarship to Buddhist teachings.[28] From this time onward scholars who regularly sought highly esteemed learned monks, including scholars whose fame is still well known today, would make a very long list. Buddhist philosophy, it would seem, took the leadership in all intellectual and theoretical circles.

The north of China was a different state of affairs. From the time that the five *Hu* Hun-Tartar[29] nations fought for hegemony over the northern Chinese plains, Buddhism received support as a force that could influence public opinion to win over and build up ethnic (non-Han) political power. When the Xiongnu tartar Shi Le (from Kashgar) was about to set up the Zhao Kingdom and himself as emperor (Zhao Chengdi, of the Liang, 345-357 CE), he hesitated three times, since he was well aware of the ancient classical tradition of China, and knew that within the literature of the Confucian classics there was no basis for finding justification for a non-Han to assume leadership or establish a kingdom on Chinese soil. But the monk from Kashgar Fuo Tu Cheng used the Buddhist theory of cause and effect, and reward of past good deeds, to support the rule of Shi Le. He brought forward the argument that in a past life Shi Le had been an ascetic Buddhist monk, and thus in the present life had merited the right to become a ruler in the land of Jin, a just and proper reason. A serious political problem was thus resolved in a simple manner.

When the Han Chinese author Lang Wang Du opposed Emperor Zhao Shi's honoring the Buddha, Shihu refuted him saying: "The Emperor was born in a border kingdom, while you, sir, were born in China. It is proper that he give honor to the Buddha, who was a holy person from Rung (i.e., non-Han origin)." His purpose was to let the tartars worship their own spirits, to protect themselves and their countries. But this attitude broke through the fetters of traditional Chinese culture, which had opposed worshipping the Buddha, bringing with it a sort of new awakening. Because of this Fuo Tu Cheng was the first monk to become a part of important military policy making, a person who from top to bottom (of society) pushed forward the development of Buddhism. From this time onward he became a model for influencing Hun political decisions. The Indo-scythian Fu Jian, who built the flourishing kingdom of Qian Qin (the Northern Liang in Shanxi) after besieging and capturing Xiangyang, took captive the noted monk Dao An, brought him back to Changan and supported him. He then conducted military campaigns as far westward as Kashgar, where he captured the famous monk Kumarajiva (ca. 384

CE). Due to changes in political fortune, Kumarajiva remained in Liangzhou for seventeen years; later, during the Hou Qin period the ruler Yao Xing welcomed him to enter Changan (401 CE).

Yao Xing's Hou Qin (the Later Qin) was a kingdom of the Jiang ethnic minority. He considered it of great importance to create good relations with the Chinese and their flourishing culture, which he did by repeatedly promoting Buddhist doctrines of reasoning. He showed the deepest respect for Kumarajiva, giving him the title "Teacher of the Nation," and organizing around him for the first time in China's history a national center for translating Buddhist texts. He invited monks from all over China, north and south of the Great River and along the upper and lower reaches of the Yellow river to come there and study. There were on an average more than 5,000 monks at any given time in Changan, greatly advancing the exchange of cultural relationships and channels of communication between all ethnic groups in the nation. "Nine out of ten" of the Hou Qin's leading intellectuals were Buddhists, bringing about a high tide of Buddhism in the northern kingdoms.

Kumarajiva's ancestors were from India. His father married a Kashgar princess, thus making him a member of the noble class. He spent his youth as a traveling scholar, visiting such places as Scythia, Kashmir, and Sogdia, and then lived for an extended length of time in Liangzhou (capital city of the Northern Liang Kingdom), a place accustomed to cultural exchanges between China and the western regions (Xinjiang). He spent eleven years in Chang'an, where he systematically introduced the thinking of the creators of the Madhyamika school, revealing internal contradictions in the theory of rational thinking, and the limits of linguistic understanding. We can see here a continuation of the influence and spread of Greek skepticism; its well defined methodology entered deeply into every school of Chinese Buddhism. Kumarajiva was honored as the founder of the

Madhyamika school of Buddhism in China. He who was at first a low and unknown novice (of the school in India) became the most renowned scholar in north and south China.

The Northern Liang was a kingdom founded by the Xiongnu tartar Ju Qu. He was addicted to a belief in spirit and medium-shamans, and was also a strong supporter of Buddhism. He had huge Buddhist statues made at Mt. Wutai, and financially aided the Indian monk Dharmaraksa translate various texts. Dharmaraksa had for a long time been active in Kusana, Tokharia, Dunhuang, and the western reaches of the Yellow River. Furthermore, fame of the spiritual wonders wrought by him spread to every kingdom within China. His translation of the *Mahasamghata Sutra*[30] and other such texts which brought a form of animism (all things have a spirit) and pantheism into Buddhism, had a relatively profound effect on the faith of the various Turkish people of the western regions. The theory of *Icchantika* appended to the last section of the *Greater Prajnaparamita Sutra*[31] which taught that all sentient beings, (even *icchantika*, i.e., non-believers) can be saved by the Bodhisattva vow, made the theory that "all sentient beings have the Buddha nature" even more popular throughout the central provinces of China.

The Northern Wei (424-532 CE) was a kingdom founded by the Xianbei (Tuoba Huns). Once they had destroyed the Liang and united north China, one could say that Buddhism had the most rapid and large scale expansion in the history of our nation, incomparable with anything before or after that time. Throughout the Northern Wei period the making of the massive Yungang and Longmen Buddhist cave carvings, the construction of magnificent ornate temples and monasteries, the casting of gilded bronze statues, the supporting of Buddhist monasteries and Stupas at public expense, show that Buddhism had in fact become the state religion. By statistical count at the end of the Northern Wei, there were 30,000 monasteries with monks and nuns numbering over 2,000,000. In Luoyang alone there were 1300 monasteries. The

Indian monks Bodhiruci (in Luoyang ca. 508 CE), Buddhasakta (524-539 CE) and Ratnamati (ca 500 CE), came to China at about this time, and resided in Luoyang, Yedu (Linzhang in Hebei) and other such places for a lengthy period, in order to organize a large scale Buddhist translation project. The greater part of their translations included the Abhidharmakosa school of Vasubandhu, its texts and theories.

Vasubandhu, founder of the Abhidharmakosa (Yogacara-idealist school) was originally from the Kingdom of Peshawar and its capital city Gandhara. Peshawar, which had inherited to a great extent its cultural traditions from Greece, had a deep and profound effect on Chinese traditional Culture. After the creation of Yogacara idealism there, the movement spread to the great monastery of Nalanta, where it became the branch of Mahayana Buddhism with the greatest authority and power. The influence of Greek idealism in Europe was also deep and long-lasting. It has effected such modern western thinkers as Baker, Kant, and Mach. In China the earliest traces and formulation of Yogacara idealism, which influenced later central Buddhist thinkers such as Faxiang can be found in the Northern Wei. The Northern Wei especially supported the position of Vasubandhu represented in his theory of the Ten Stages, as enunciated in the *Dasabhumi Sutra*[32] (*The Ten Stages*, 52 steps for becoming a Bodhisattva). Due to this support the power of the Ten Stage school became very great. It produced people of great talent and a very high level of scholarly learning, making it difficult for (scholars of) the southern kingdoms to do more than trail far behind in the distance.

Buddhism continued to develop and expand during the Northern Qi and the Northern Zhou. The Ten Stage Bodhisattva school continued to have a unifying effect on all of the other schools. During the Northern Qi Han Chinese held political power, though the land itself came under the Xianbei (Tuoba) Huns. The Northern Zhou was a rule of both Tuoba and Wenbu

Tartars (Huns). In summation, the Five Hun kingdoms all promoted Buddhism, with the Xianbei (Northern Wei) as the foundation stone of support.

The fact that Buddhism spread so broadly and quickly in the northern kingdoms had a deep and lasting effect on the south. The monk Buddhatrata from North India received the support of men like Liu Yu, who set up a project for the translation of Buddhist texts during the Qin-Song periods. Together with Faxian he translated the *Mahaprajna Nirvana Sutra*,[33] the first occurrence of a theory not in accord with the original Prajna teaching. It taught that "enlightenment does not occur when desires are eliminated; the Buddha is the true self, and all sentient beings have the Buddha nature." This single point shook to their roots all of the leading Buddhist intellectuals and their surroundings, and historically was an event on which all subsequent Chinese Buddhist schools were based. It became the kernel of the Nirvana school's teachings on the Buddha nature, penetrating eventually into the entire world of Chinese thought.

From the time of Song Wen Di (424-453 CE), who took Buddhism as a way of "governing by peaceful sitting (meditation)," a special art attributed to it in the south, Buddhism in the southern kingdoms became a method for political rule and thought control. Because of this the character of Buddhism in the kingdoms where Han Chinese dominated, also changed. From another aspect, the political rulers' support of Buddhism provided the conditions for its development and creativity. The Liang-Sung courts supported the monk Gunabhadra who came from central India (435-468 CE) to continue the work of translation. Among his translations are the *Srimalya Sutra*[34] which first mentioned the important concept of the "Tathagata Storehouse," the *Lankavatara Sutra*[35] which introduced the notion of "Alaya" consciousness of the idealist school's system, and the *Sutra of Twelve Penitential Acts*[36] which promoted the idea of ascetic penance. Basically, the "Lankavatara Masters" and penitents who practiced and developed these translations, were for the most part active in north China. They were the precursors of the Tang dynasty's Chan school. The "Tathagata Storehouse" was an explanation of the Buddha Nature, which with the prior translation by Faxiang's "stilling the heart-mind" concept, became an important theory of Chinese Buddhism on the intellect.

The Qi and Liang periods were the apex of Buddhism in the south of China, but translation projects by this time had slacked off. During the Liang-Chen periods the Western Indian monk Paramartha came from the southern route into China (ca. 546 CE). He was rejected by the noble class and high ranking monks, and never received the support of the political authorities. Drifting from place to place for more than twenty years, he translated and introduced the works of the Yoga school and its scriptures. That which he taught, for the most part, was from the *Mahayana Samparigraha Sastra*,[37] (the "Concentration of Mind"). His formation of the "Concentration of Mind" school spread from Guangzhou northward, blending with and influencing the Ten Stage Bodhisattva school of northern Buddhism. Finally, after the unification of China and its two capitals, these theories had a deep and penetrating effect on Buddhism during the Sui-Tang periods (561-906 CE). The phrase "Not a speck of dust falls on Idealism" defined its definitive role as the presupposition of all Chinese Buddhist schools and their theories.

In summation, during the two Jin periods, the Sixteen Kingdoms, and the North-South periods the major force promoting Buddhism was that of the five Tungusic-Hun rulers, representing China's minority ethnic people. The influence of Buddhist thought from abroad, in a constant and unbroken line of transmission, continued to penetrate to every corner of society. Tides of new thought came pouring in to China, including the Madhyamika, Nirvana, Abhidharmakosa, Theravada, Lankavatara, Dasabhumi, Samparigraha, and the Dhyana (Zen) scriptures, their masters and schools. These new ideas were like blades of grass springing up after a spring rain, emerging in an endless stream. They created vast territories of Buddhist dominated lands and enriched the innermost reaches of cultural and intellectual life.

What is most noteworthy is that during this period in China the ethnic question was quite complicated. Only Buddhism was able to mediate and bring solutions to the strife between various ethnic groups. It was the most important link in bringing together various ethnic peoples. E.g., Shi Zhao Zeng from Tashkent had a most discriminatory policy against minorities, but he was the first to promulgate a freedom of religion policy for Han and minority peoples (due to Buddhist influence). The Northern Wei had the longest period and broadest scope of Buddhist rule. But it did not due to this become any less Chinese. To the contrary, it quickly reached the highest level of sinicization. Zeng Lang who was born in Jingzhao, lived on Mt. Tai during the Fu Qin period. The common people came to him in great numbers, bringing gold to be accepted as his disciples, and waited in long lines in front and behind him to be invited into his entourage. Nobles and kings bequeathed him noble rank and titles to feudal land. Besides Fu Jian, these included Morong Jun of Qian Yan, Yao Xing of the later Qin, Chiba Gui the Tuoba ruler of Wei, and Xiao Wu Di the ruler of Eastern Jin. Thus from a small coterie of more or less 100 monks, he soon became a central force for uniting all sorts of ethnic groups and nations. Taking the example again of Dao An, the western regions (Xinjiang) honored him with the title "Bodhisattva of the Eastern Regions." When he left the northern kingdoms, he was welcomed by the Court of the Eastern Jin, and on his frequent returns to Chang'an, he has called the honored guest of the former Qin. There are innumerable examples such as those mentioned above. Buddhism by reason of its wealth of ideas was a source of uninterrupted friendly relationships, structuring and uniting the feelings and intellectual exchanges between ethnic groups, enriching their life and customs, and bringing a common religious-cultural psychology. We must admit that Buddhism was the most positive factor in merging the cultures of other ethnic groups with the Han during the Northern Wei.

III

The formation of the various Buddhist schools of the Sui-Tang period (581-906 CE) is considered to be the completion of the sinicization of Buddhism in China. The reason for this is because the schools of the period were formed by ethnically Han Chinese who had further distanced themselves from Buddhism coming from abroad. Actually such a statement shows a serious lack of familiarity concerning the reality of Chinese Buddhism.

Of all of the Buddhist schools established during the Sui-Tang period, only two were founded by ethnically Han Chinese, i.e. the Tiantai and the Three Stage schools. The Tiantai school based its teachings on the Lotus Sutra *Saddharma-pundarika sutra*,[38] a title coming from abroad. The texts of the Three Stage school, (founded by the monk Xinxing in the Sui Dynasty, it was proscribed in 600 and 725 CE, ed. note) were mostly self-created. Repeatedly interdicted, it was finally wiped out in the Tang Dynasty. Except for these two cases, there was not a single school founded during the Sui-Tang that did not have close relations with non-Han monks. Not only did (the new sects and non-Han monks) have continuing support from the feudal government of the nation, but their mixed socio-religious characteristics were in a special way suitable to the needs of society. They allowed Chinese Buddhist philosophy to reach entirely new intellectual heights. Let us examine these developments according to diachronic occurrence:

The earliest founder of Madhyamika Buddhism (in China) was the monk Jizang. He was of Parthian origin. His ancestors took refuge in China, where he was born in the city of Jinling

(Nanjing) which was the criterion for saying that he was an "old immigrant" (born outside of China). Thus he was also called "Tungusic (Hun) Jizang." His influence, from the time of his birth, extended through four dynasties, the Liang, Chen, Sui, and Tang. He passed through many hardships, having experienced fully the ups and downs (heat and cold) of the contemporary world. Yet all of the personal hardships he experienced were in the context of high ranking monks and court nobles, under the support of the royal court and officials of succeeding dynasties. Such experiences could not have any other than a definitive role and function in the formulation of his thought.

When Jizang was still a child he took the vows of a monk, as a disciple of Falang. Falang was a great Madhyamika master of the Mt. She hillside monastery (near Nanjing). From the time of Emperor Wu of the Liang, the Mahayana and the Satyasiddhi Sutras[39] had come to be held in the highest esteem, and were the foremost school in evidence throughout the southern kingdoms. By the Chen dynasty, Madhyamika had become the school of thought most trusted by the Imperial Household, officials, and nobles. All of those who became monks and studied it advanced rapidly in their careers. When Falang was brought to the capital and put in charge of the court temple, the realist school of Madhyamika reached the pinnacle of its influence. Jizang came forth precisely at the time when Madhyamika had reached the highest level of eminence. He was nineteen years old when due to his keen skills at debate and exposition he was brought to the Chen court at Yangzhou. When the Chen kingdom was destroyed (587 CE) Emperor Xing's court sponsored Madhyamika suffered a serious blow. The eminent monks all fled. Jizang went eastward to Mt. Kuaiji, where he dwelt in the Jiaxiang temple of Mt. Qin Wang for more than ten years. Here he received more than 1,000 novices and monks as disciples. From the beginning to the end of the Sui Dynasty, when Yang Guang Jin was Prince Regent, he was called to Changan where he began the golden years of his life.

The major text used by him at this time was the *Vimalakirti Nirdesa Sutra*, thus attacking and striking a mortal blow to the Southern Dynasties' Satyasiddhi sect (a Theravada version of the *Sunya* or Madhyamika school). The story has it that Xi Wang Xian opened the scriptures before all of his disciples, and asked Jizang to take the podium and explain it. He thereupon defeated the monk Seng An, who was a proponent of the Ten Step Bodhisattva school (*Dasabhumi Sutra*). He opened and explained the Lotus Sutra (Saddharma-pundarika Sutra). Word of this traveled with the winds, and thousands came to listen to his teachings. "The powerful clans and noble classes brought him their gold, and donated their accumulated wealth, needing a myriad coffers to store it." Amidst the devastation and evil wrought by the Sui Dynasty, Jizang spent his time carving some 25 Buddhist statues, as a way of causing all to whole heartedly repent. He further erected a statue and cult to the Bodhisattva Samantabhadra, opposing dhyana (*Chan*) concentration, and holding that contemplating reality (as opposed to an absolute) was an empty theory.

Upon the accession of the Tang Dynasty, he was appointed as a teacher in the capital. The Sangha of monks urged Jizang to speak to Li Yuan (the first Tang Emperor), which he did, saying, "The four levels of society (scholar, farmer, artisan, merchant) are all weak and impoverished. Take advantage of this opportunity to save the weak and miserable masses. People look up to you and rely on your help. Look around the sea and the sky with mercy!" This kind of attitude truly moved the new emperor and his court deeply. The event was recorded in the biographies of famous monks as one of the ten greatest acts of virtue of the entire nation, during the Tang Dynasty.

Dao Xuan wrote a critique in praise of Jizang as follows: "He was trusted by all around him, and unceasingly did a storehouse of good things," a truly profound assessment. Jizang saw neither good or bad in natural events, made no judgment of should or should not in politics, saw through the red dust and bitter loneliness of worldly affairs, cast off to the utmost any sensuous desires or petty disputes, and was able to tolerate even the lowest form of difficulty and shame. It would seem that almost all of the monks who expounded Madhyamika theory since the Liang-Chen periods were offspring of the rich and noble. Jizang was especially outspoken against accumulating wealth. Receiving the patronage of emperors such as Chen Shubao and Yang Guang in the declining period of their reign, he as able to deeply influence the social nature of the Madhyamika sect.

Jizang was the monk with the greatest influence on Buddhist thinking of his time. The special contribution and emphasis of his thought was to explain and rectify the popular double truth principle of Buddhist philosophy, i.e., the *samvrti-satya* theory that there is a vulgar truth for ordinary people, and an enlightened truth *paramartha-satya* for the monk. In Jizang's view, both kinds of knowledge were considered to be the same, i.e., he changed "double truth" to "both kinds of satya knowledge are relative." This was a great change from early Buddhist thought. The double truth theory was formulated by an earlier form of Buddhist thinking to coordinate the contradiction between saving people who lived in the ordinary world, and those who left the world to be monks. The truth for the enlightened the *Paramartha satya* taught was that "all Buddhist teachings are empty," an absolute, higher form of truth. Ordinary knowledge, i.e., knowledge proper to the ordinary world or *samvrti-satya* teaches that "nature/form is empty," a kind of truth or understanding directed towards the salvation of all sentient beings. Thus Buddhism recognizes a lesser sort of *upaya* convenient skillful means, i.e., a relative sort of truth for ordinary beings. This kind of double truth was the basis of official Liang Dynasty Buddhist teaching. Its premises and conclusion created two kinds of social realities. Those who lived in the world and those who lived apart from it were two opposite poles.

Jizang criticized this sort of thinking. He felt that both kinds of thought were relative, not absolute. It is because one takes all sentient beings to be distinct, sickness and disease to be different, that there can be two kinds of truth. Only by reason of a change in teaching can there be two truths, i.e,, the two truths depend on how truth is taught. The two truths are effective only in a determined context of thought, and thus he called them both "relative truths." Therefore the two "truths" do not depend upon reason for their being, but rather on words used in linguistic or epistemological teaching, with the meaning assigned to them arbitrarily by the teacher. Absolute reason or thought itself cannot be divided, cannot be spoken, cannot indeed be conceptualized. Thus one cannot arrive at any affirmation or denial of a concrete or real thing. To leave the world and to be in the world are concepts derived from teaching or learning words, i.e., epistemological values. Thus teaching or learning names for things is arbitrary, not absolute, nor can it ever attain to an absolute. Therefore speaking from basics, to distinguish this shore from that shore, Buddha nature from the *chantika* i.e., those who are without desire for salvation, nirvana from the realm of life and death, is impossible. Jizang called his methodology "Cutting off 100 evils with four words." Arguments cannot be carried on endlessly; they soon exceed myriads of words. In the end all they gain is human misunderstanding (men not knowing what they talk about). The original meaning of theory itself is something that cannot be ultimately defined or denied. If one takes this kind of viewpoint as a concrete methodology and uses it in one's own daily life, then in training the body and nourishing one's inner self, there is "nothing to be attained." "To attain to nothing" (absolute, other shore) is for the Madhyamika school the highest realm of achievement. Such an attitude is one in which the distinction between honor and disgrace, gain and loss, do not bring emotional attachment or upset. Such an ability to keep internal peace and detachment whether receiving the highest honor or the lowest disgrace is indeed difficult to attain.

Due to frequent changes in class structure and the accompanying shift in political power, rapid switches from poverty to riches and nobility to commoners was of frequent occurrence in China's feudal social situation. The classical philosophy which is perhaps closest to expressing the decline in morals and feelings of crisis and fear that come at the end of an epoch is the *Liezi*. But when it comes to choosing a philosophy that boosts morals during a crisis that of Jizang is by far the richest and deepest. His philosophy provides an excellent summary criticism of the social disorder and indulgence in sensual pleasure that was typical of the spirit of the times. If the words of the sages are only used to instruct the benighted masses in abstract principles of truth, what power indeed does the sage have? What power does the teaching of (philosophical) names have to convince? The Madhyamika school began to lose its power and prestige from the time of Tai Zong (the second Tang Emperor). Its followers were scattered to the four directions, because the new emperor did not like its emotional appeal and tendencies. Madhyamika no longer exists in China as a real force which can unify monastic organizations. But its critical attitude towards the times and its penetrating philosophy in a period filled with dissatisfaction, sought to pierce deeply into the old attitudes of belief of the people. Its influence was deep and long-lasting.

The kind of religious philosophy that Tang Tai Zong sought, however, was one with a more positive and practical response to the world (of his time) and the human condition. Of all the schools functioning in the country at the time that he could have selected, it was quite by any caprice that he chose to bring forth and support the monk Xuanzang, who had traveled abroad to study Buddhism. Xuanzang was the earliest ancestor of the Faxiang Yogacara school. He was ethnically and by birth most decidedly Han Chinese, but theoretically (by training) his doctrines were totally foreign. Because of his foreign experiences, he was not that much in line with national conditions, and his reading of the religious pulse was insufficient. But most importantly, he scrupulously followed the teachings of his masters, including the so-called "five kinds of nature" theory. He felt that if there was the slightest presence of emotional attachment, the Buddha nature could not be present. He also taught that by nature the heart-mind is impure. This was out of line with the ordinarily accepted theory in China that nature was basically pure. Concerning all those who in later years criticized Xuanzang for this, the most important thing to note is that this theory derives from doctrines taught by disciples who came much after him, a possible widespread and long-standing misunderstanding of what he actually believed.

Xuanzang's translations obviously included the "Five Kinds of Nature" texts, but these passages were not truly representative of his own personal beliefs (i.e., things he himself personally emphasized). In the *Vidyamatra-siddhi Sastra*[40] that he translated and annotated, there is not even the slightest mention of the doctrine that beings that have emotions or feelings do not have the Buddha nature, and thus cannot become a Buddha or achieve enlightenment. On the contrary, he divided the Buddha nature into two kinds, the *li* rational, and *zhi* intuitive or direct Buddha nature. All sentient beings have the *li* rational nature, while only a few have the wisdom nature, which is different according to each individual case. He emphasized the twofold doctrine of consciousness, *benyou* that one had by origin, and *shiqi* that which arises afterwards. He promoted the doctrine that the original alaya consciousness is perfumed by seeds that brought forth knowledge, i.e., he did not make having or producing thought a hardened or predetermined thing. Therefore, theoretically, one cannot arrive at the conclusion that he personally taught that not all sentient beings can attain the Buddha nature. The purpose of Xuanzang in going to India was obviously to solve difficult problems concerning the theory of the Buddha nature, including whether "things that do not have human nature, but have feelings and sensations" can or cannot participate in the Buddha nature. Another concern was whether or not one could attain the Buddha nature without having gone through a period of self-cultivation and discipline. According to the authoritative *Biography of Master Sanzang, Master of the Da Ci En Temple*,[41] the ultimate answer obtained by Xuanzang in India had to be completely accepted, and could not be opposed.

Of course by such evidence we cannot arrive at a concrete proof of what Xuanzang's own discourses actually contained. The two contradictory legends (whether or not Xuanzang taught that all sentient beings had the Buddha nature, or whether a period of discipline was required to realize the Buddha nature) were perhaps all due to the sectarian feelings and emotions of his later disciples. They cannot be used as an example to prove Xuanzang's own thought. At the point that Xuanzang proposed the theory that the mind could by nature be sullied from within, (Alaya consciousness and seed of consciousness theory), it is a fact that this did not coincide with the currently popular "theory of mind" school. In later days the theory of "original nature" and "functioning nature" were quite by accident taken to be consistent with the viewpoint of the second Tang Emperor Tai Zong, who vigorously supported the usefulness for all sides to define human nature, an extraordinary boost (for Xuanzang).

There was a much deeper reason why Xuanzang's Dharma Laksana idealism was selected by a feudal dynasty which was filled with a spirit of vitality and progress. At the core of the *Vidyamatrasiddhi Sutra*[42] is the theory that "there is only mind, no reality," an idea deriving from the basic assumption that everything can change, (i.e., from the *laksana* six accompanying forms of reality, i.e., whole and part, together and separate, integral and disparate). The term "everything can change" refers to the dynamic power of the mind to initiate subjective activity, to create. The theory of *laksana* or accompanying forms explains how to recognize that the very notion of objectivity comes from a subjective relationship, i.e., the mind recognizes that in each case reality is different (i.e., the very act of recognizing objective reality in in each subjective mind is itself relative and different). This standpoint completely accounted for the formal structure of ultra-idealism. Moreover as far as strengthening belief in the ability to improve one's own personal life and power of creativity, this Buddhist school more than any other had a positive effect on influencing the ideas of a monarch of great talent and vision, a more logical way of keeping with the times.

Nevertheless in the final analysis the only reason why Xuanzang's teachings were able to develop into a school was because of the activities of his disciples. Broadly speaking, his followers divided into two branches. The first, which took Kui Ji as its head, was called the *Ci En* (Compassionate Reward) school, while the second which took Yuan Ce as its leader, was considered to be heretical by the *Ci En* school. Neither of these leaders was of Han ethnic origin.

Kui Ji was of noble origin. His secular surname was Weichi. According to the Sung dynasty *Biography of Famous Monks*,[43] his ancestors can be traced to the later Wei period. Since his surnam was Weichi, it follows that he must have been of Xian Bei (Tartar) ethnic origin. He was a disciple of Xuanzang, from head to toe a lofty and eminent person. In view of the above facts (of Xuanzang's appeal), having personally seen the differences in each of the other great Buddhist masters i.e., the (Sravana) "Many Sages of the Five Heavens," he was convinced that Xuanzang's theories alone were insufficient. He strongly advised Xuanzang to change his style of study from solely translating scriptures to one that included practice. Thus he could provide a concrete model to the critical eye for distinguishing the true from the false. Kui Ji thus convinced Xuanzang to edit another book more suitable to be adapted by those who were discussing and also wished to practice the ideas expressed in his great works. Xuanzang accepted this idea, and the result was the *Cheng Wei Shi Lun*.[44] This explains how even though Xuanzang's school of Buddhist learning most decidedly came from India, still much of the contents of his writings were his own work.

Kui Ji's expounding of Xuanzang's doctrines had many results, the most important of which were the promulgation of the doctrines of the "Three Kinds of Buddhist realms" (*yu*, real, *kong* empty, and *zhong* middle stages), and the theory of Buddha Nature. The "Three Kinds of Realms" are derived from the distinction between objective and subjective understanding, and the relationship between these two mental states, i.e., perceived nature, emotion, and the material realm. This kind of viewpoint had an enriching effect on the various theories of cognition. The debates on the Buddha Nature that Kui Ji engaged in supported the theory of the "five kinds of Buddha Nature," and received the greatest amount of opposition. The truth was that he had developed this theory from Xuanzang's "two kinds of Buddha Nature," using the "power of wisdom" to explain the difference in higher and lower forms of sentient beings as a radical difference in nature. This way of thinking was quite close to the Confucian distinction between higher forms of wisdom and a lower vulgar mentality, a view that reinforced the superiority complex of the noble classes and learned monks. Yet it differed greatly from discriminatory materials used by those outside Buddhist circles to fan the flames of religious discrimination. Besides the above, he also urged that free rein be given to the kind of reasoning expounded in the Hetuvidya texts, (i.e., the science of causality and logical reasoning). He particularly expounded the correct method of explaining the *paramartha* true categories of reality, causing this method of reasoning, along with other Buddhist methods of logic already current, to be held in even higher esteem, making them active and vibrant for an even lengthier period of time.

Yuan Ce was the grandson of the Ruler of the New Luo Kingdom, of Korean ancestry. It is not clear when he came to China. He was thirteen years younger than Xuanzang. He grew up in basically the same sort of cultural background as Xuanzang who had been deeply tainted by the older form of Yogacara translations. Thus when the new translations of Xuanzang were received, he had the deepest respect for their "True Realization" (*paramartha*) teaching. A number of the older Paramartha texts are preserved in his work entitled *The Sutra Explaining the Deepest Mysteries*,[45] all of which are concerned with introducing (Paramartha) objective thought, by the method of "achieving mastery by a comprehensive study of the subject." That which he laid most emphasis on spreading was the *Vidya Matrasiddhi Sastra*. Men of later times passed on a story about him saying that he secretly slipped in and listened to the master's discourses, arriving before Kui Ji began the lesson, but did not "bow his head" as did the others to be accepted as Kui Ji's disciple, in order to talk to him personally. However it is a fact that Yuan Ce lived in the Xi Ming Temple under Abbot Dao Xuan, who with most of his monks did not get along well with the Ci En temple where Kui Ji lived. Afterwards Yuan Ce took part in a variety of temple translation projects, and ended his years in China. At the end of the northern Song Dynasty (1128 CE), a new pagoda was built by someone in his honor, in which his remains and those of Kui Ji were put on an equal level next to the pagoda dedicated to Xuanzang, a fact that reflects how he was critically esteemed in later generations.

Kui Ji's teachings spread to Japan, while Yuan Ce's were brought to Korea. Thus the influence of both men had an international character. The influence of Xuanzang's teachings is still felt within China, where his fame has not come to an end. From the early Song Dynasty onward his school of thought became one with that of Chan (Zen) where it lives on and flourishes. Yogacara Idealism must be taken as one of the most important schools in

China, especially within the context of training young monks and novices. During the Yuan period northern and southern Chan, Yogacara, Tiantai and Xianshou (Huayan) teachings were considered to be the most important for becoming a monk. From the Ming Dynasty onward there was a new development, i.e., not only was Yogacara Idealism respected by the monks, but it also became an important element within the intellectual official class, especially within the various schools of Neo-confucianism. whose thinkers held it in deepest respect.

The founder of the *Xian Shou* or *Huayan* school was Fazang, whose ancestors were from outside of China. His ascendants were registered as immigrants from Sogdiana, and thus he was given the title *Kangzang*, "Sogdian Zang." When still very young he left his family and went to Mt. Zhongnan (in Shaanxi province), to study Buddhism.

Mt. Zhongnan had been a center of Avatamsaka Sutra teaching since the Zhou and Sui periods (Sixth century CE). The monks of the Huayan persuasion for the most part went through rough and bumpy times. It is said that due to suffering and cruelty, some of them even committed suicide. Chang'an was just over the mountains from Mt. Zhongnan. News and information came back and forth over the mountain quickly. Among the many learned monks was a spirit that fostered independence in thinking, and created a new and brave atmosphere of creativity. Fazang's teacher Zhiyan (Fourth Patriarch of Hua yen teachings, 600-668 CE) had a change in fortune, when due to a memorial he was embraced by the court. This gave Fazang free access to the capital and the court, where he came into contact with the highest classes. Thus the Huayan religious-philosophical system quickly gained imperial favor and recognition. From this we can understand his widespread fame, which of course was based on solid causes.

After the death of the Second Tang Emperor Tai Zong, the western regions (today's Xinjiang) developed serious border problems. The stabilizing of Khotan, which had always had close connections with the interior of China, was of special strategic significance. Historically Khotan had been Buddhist for some time. It is said that one of the monks who spread Buddhism there was an Arhat named after Vairocana (the Bright Sun Buddha). The Zan Mo Temple which was built in honor of him was famous even inside China proper. Almost all historical sources record his presence.

The *Avatamsaka Sutra*[46] was not from India, but was collated into a sutra in Khotan. The main Buddha honored in the Sutra is not Sakyamuni (the historical Buddha), but is Vairocana or Rocana (Buddha as sunlight, and fire, respectively). Due to this Tang Gao Zong (650-684 CE) and Empress Wu Zetian (684-705 CE) supported the Huayan sutra, a decision that cannot be seen as arbitrary. When the great Vairocana statue at Lungmen Caves was made in 672 CE, Empress Wu contributed 20,000 strings of cash. Two years later Sun Simiao memorialized Emperor Gao Zong to have the Huayan Sutra given equally high rank with the Prajna-paramita Sutra. In 695 CE the Empress Wu requested Fazang to give lessons in the Huayan sutra, and at the same time sent a messenger to Khotan inviting the monk Siksananda to bring an original copy of the Avatamsaka text to Luoyang to be retranslated. The translation project was of very high standard, in no way inferior to that of Xuanzang. This was a way of showing respect for the Khotanese, and at the same time was a kind of political movement.

From the time of Empress Wu Zetian, the Tang Dynasty saw military affairs as a kind of battle against spirits and demons. As early as 675 CE the Tang imperial and provincial capitals had a temple named *Sha Mon*. *Sha Mon* is a sobriquet or title referring to the Tantric Buddhist Spirit Bishamon, guardian of the northern heavens, who was honored and favored by the

Khotanese. Buddhism made him into a spirit protector of the Dharma, and patron-protector for military affairs. When Empress Wu of (her own dynastic title) Zhou attacked the Qitan tartars, she ordered her troops into battle under the title "Shen Bing Dao" (Troops of the Spirit Way); when she attacked the Turfan Turks in the eighth month, she addressed her troops by the title "Tian Bing Dao" (Troops of the Heavenly Way). The Tang court's use of religion in this way was done under the background of the importance given to the Huayan sutra.

The basic tenets of Huayan Philosophy went far beyond Prajna and Yogacara thought. The "One heart-mind" which it attributed to all sentient beings, united reason, wisdom, and Buddha as one and the same thing, i.e., one with the basic stuff of the cosmos and the myriad creatures. It held that the original cause and the matter of the cosmos, along with all the spatial and temporal aspects of the myriad things within it, were both distinct and one, and that its unity was absolute. This sort of relationship it called "no obstacle or hindrance between thought and thing," (unimpeded interaction between noumenon and phenomenon). Every point of individuation (division) must derive from the categories imposed by mind on the non-differentiated state of phenomenon and noumenon. At the same time, all things interpenetrate all other things, and influence the condition of other things. This kind of relationship between concrete things is called "no obstacle between thing and thing" (unimpeded interaction between noumenon and noumenon). If this is so, then all individual things are infinitely involved in each other. All sorts of forms are united as one. The entire cosmos basically interpenetrates each individual nature, thus becoming united as one sum total. The Huayan use of such a viewpoint to examine and unify all phenomena was called "the genesis of the Dharma world, the cause of endless arising."

The Huayan theory that all things mutually rely on each other for existence, i.e., mutually influence and interpenetrate each other, especially its recognition that individual natures exist, and its acceptance of this as the starting point for uniting all things, is a phenomenon scarcely ever found in the history of Chinese philosophy. The point of departure for the theory was the emphasis on each nature's necessary participation in a common nature, due to which it necessarily follows that nature itself was entirely interpenetrated by the absolute, (transcendent, i.e., that which is outside of space). This sort of thinking had a deep and all-pervading influence on northern and southern Song Dynasty rationalism (960-1281 CE).

The theory of the Huayan school from the time of its inception until its maturation was itself a sort of process philosophy that went in step with the unification of the various peoples of north China, and the pacification and unification of the entire nation. Fazang's intellectual restructuring of Huayan made it a colorful and flourishing system that mututally influenced and illuminated Chinese and non-Han peoples alike, making it easy for people of the racially diverse Tang period to think alike, bringing about a period of true peace and equality between different ethnic groups and social classes.

The two most powerful schools of the Tang Dynasty were Tantric Buddhism and Chan (Zen). Their special characteristics are well known and studied, and thus are not the subject of explanation in this article. What must be explained, however, is the route that tantric Buddhism took on its entrance into China. The most important point to emphasize here is that its place of origin was south India and Sri Lanka. From there it passed through Java and the influence of an ethnically Austronesian people, and then only in later times did it reach Chang'an in China. It brought with it the religious countenance and ethnic customs of the southern, i.e., the water silk route, including a certain amount of Indian popular religion. Because of the military needs of the far western reaches of the Yellow River region, especially from the time of the An Lu Shan rebellion (752 CE), Tantric Buddhism became the Buddhist Dharma Way of protecting the army, the nation, and the individual body. The Tang rulers looked to it with high hopes that it might become the most influential religious sect of the time. However, due to the opposition to Buddhism that developed from the mid Tang period onward (i.e., Emperor Wu's interdiction of Buddhism, 845-847 CE), it fell from power. However from the time that the Tang Emperor Dai Zong (763-780 CE) proposed that the monk Amogha (Bu Kong, Yu Chao En) translate the *Ren Wong Hu Guo* Sutra,[47] Tantric Buddhism had great influence in many monasteries, and was transmitted continuously over a number of dynastic reign eras.

The situation of Chan Buddhism was a bit more complicated. We will not discuss the social basis or the thought tendencies of the many Chan schools that developed during the Tang and Song periods. So many changes occurred that it would be impossible to put all our conclusions about them "in a single basket." But there is one point that can be affirmed here, i.e to say that it is a totally Han creation does not tally with reality. Of course we will not claim that its founder was the Indian or Parthian monk Bodhidharma. Historically there were at least three Bodhidharma of this sort. But if we simply look at Hui Neng, the claimed founder of the southern Chan sect, Hung Ren, i.e., Zhi Chi, they were said to be of Yao ethnic origin, a sign at least of how deeply the ethnic minorities had penetrated into the monasteries of China. In Sichuan one of the Chan masters with the greatest influence was Jing Zhong, of the Bao Tang branch of Chan. Thus at least one of its founders was born in the new Luo Kingdom of Wu Xiang. Out of respect he was called the "Golden Monk."

Thus the single basic factor in the birth and daily life of Buddhism that did not change, the single condition that remained the same amidst the many and variegated aspects of Buddhism's development, the unifying feature in all of the schools that were gestated from its fertile depths, all were influenced in any number of diverse ways by ethnic minorities, i.e., non-Han monks. Furthermore, the creative living power of these minority people is still visible. It would be totally out of context to claim that Buddhism was totally a Han Chinese movement, even in the most Chinese of Buddhist eras.

IV

When Buddhism from abroad entered into the interior of China, it brought about changes not only in the reshaping of ancient Chinese cultural thought, but also a new sort of structural transformation in society and politics as well. This sort of change was mainly apparent in the formation of monastic communities with their various levels of monks, and the strength that Buddhism provoded beyond just existing to buffer strong opposition from society outside itself.

From the time that the monks and their monastic communities first appeared in China, they adopted a policy of not asking about worldly affairs -- more importantly, they never inquired into the political aspects of worldly affairs. They formulated this plan in order to avoid dictatorial government interference and control over their internal affairs, and to preserve the freedom to pursue any kind of individual thought and private activities. This is the so-called *jie tuo*, i.e., casting off or total separation from worldly affairs. Because of a mutual positive response, they asked the nation to recognize Buddhism as an independent reality, thus preserving the monks' right to ask for self-reliant status. Because of this, the power of Buddhism increased day-by-day to new heights. By the time of Hui Yuan in the Eastern Jin dynasty (317-419 CE), this kind of tendency led to a movement that exempted Buddhists from attending court ritual.

The Eastern Jin had many instances of monks meeting to discuss this problem. It was decided that a certain number of monks should be appointed to offer their respects and bring the question to the King. Hui Yuan was sent as a representative to clear up the matter at court, i.e., to see if all must be brought together to reach an agreement about the religious ritual system, which would protect imperial authority. I.e., was it necessary for the monks to leave the monastery, while respectfully observing national rituals according to law?

A group of monks with Hui Yuan as their spokesperson supported by another group of officials, were against this this kind of integration. Hui Yuan wrote his treatise *On Monks not offering ritual to the Ruler*,[48] in which he argued that the world was divided into two sorts of people, those who lived in the world, and those who lived apart from it. Buddhism too he divided into two parts, believers who lived in the world, and monks who lived apart. Believers who lived in the world were endowed with *qi* life energy from two sources, i.e., their bodily form was from their parents, while their virtue and wisdom were from nature and the ruler. Therefore they must offer respect to parents and ruler. Those who leave their home and the world, on the contrary, see their body as a source of suffering, and because of this they no longer value life (birthing), and do not follow nature's changes. Therefore they need not express thanks to parents, nature, or ruler, nor observe such ritual obligation. Hui Yuan insisted:[49]

> All those who leave the world live in seclusion, and seek to perfect their will. They leave the world to approach the Dharma. If they go back on these goals, then they must observe worldly ritual and its customs. Those who live in seclusion must live in accord with the highest, totally different set of rules.

The result of the debate was that the monks were victorious. Buddhism in dividing and changing the centralizing tendency of feudal society, took one of the greatest steps forward in its history, symbolizing that the Sangha of Buddhist monks had already formed a special high ranking level within society, an even more important concept.

The road open to China's intellectual officials was a very narrow and restricted one. Within their intellectual environment production and technical advances were looked down upon. There were only two paths available to them, i.e., either the political road of being an official "guest" (assigned to a province away from home), or else the way of casting aside official life and returning to the fields and a life of retirement and relaxation. The career of officialdom was filled with competition and strife. Opportunities were limited and retirement was a retreat from opposing political views and disappointments within officialdom. The Qin Dynasty (221 - 206 BCE) did not allow retired officials to live, because retirement showed an attitude of non-cooperation. The intelligentsia of the Western and Eastern Han periods (206 BCE - 220 CE) persisted, and even though almost all of them chose to be "guests" (i.e., officials), some of them chose freedom and self-cultivation. The retired could get out of office to cultivate and farm the fields, but had to show unconditional support for the ruling government of the time and rely solely on the premises of the past.

When Buddhism appeared, the situation changed. It gave to those who did not want to be officials the right to choose, like Hui Yuan, the theory of leaving the world. It also created a "guest outside of society," n.b., outside the *fang* or official four quarters of city life, i.e., outside of the four accepted social groups (scholar, farmer, artisan, merchant). They organized a new legally accepted social group of monks, and also established a way of begging for food, a basically simple way of life. They used this as a way of escaping politics, and going against the commands of the ruler, a state of affairs quite different from the past.

It is said that the first Han Chinese to become a monk was Yan Futiao, during the reign of Emperor Huan of the Han Dynasty (147-168 CE). From his work the *Wise Sayings in Ten Chapters*[50] there is no question but that he was a highly cultured and literate person. During the Han-Wei period there were two princely level ministers who became monks, Guang Ling and Peng Cheng. We know that they were of high ministerial rank because of the term *xiang* (high minister) used in their titles. They were representative of the highest literate official class. With the fall of the Eastern Han (220 CE) and the sense of loss and instability that came with it, Buddhism provided for the official gentry a new path, both materially and spiritually quite different from anything open to officials who had fallen from power in the past. These monks of a different sort who were now teaching and preaching the Buddhist scriptures, were a link in the process of formulating Buddhism, which gradually developed into larger and smaller groups of monks, who eventually were organized into monastic communities. During the Three Kingdoms period Buddhist rules and vows gradually became accepted, showing clearly that this sort of Buddhist community was increasing daily. The founding of monasteries was in fact necessary to preserve law and order. Due to natural and man made disasters, and changes in governmental order and policy, groups of Buddhist organized communities of monks spread everywhere, bringing order and stability to unsettled places.

Even though the government sponsored some Buddhist groups, even to the extent of building and supporting monasteries, still the livelihood of the monks in the beginning was not peaceful or settled. Dao An was a first disciple of Fuo Tu Cheng. Afterwards, when he disappeared into the northern mountains, 400 or 500 monks followed him. After this he went south, with a great number of monks, and was welcomed by the Eastern Jin at Xiangyang. Xi Zhuochi wrote a letter to Xie An saying that Dao An's disciples numbered in the hundreds, and that he taught them endlessly without tiring. He did not use magic techniques to delude people, did not seek power or fame. His disciples who were very serious, intelligent, and came in great numbers, had nothing but praise and respect for him. Dao An remained there for fifteen years, receiving financial support and respect from officials, nobles and the court alike. The Emperor Fu Qin himself made frequent gifts. The scholar officials who entered this circle of monks could immediately escape from political circles and their control, not only avoiding harm and suffering, but also becoming a strong force opposing political struggle.

Coming to the time of Hui Yuan (ca. 402 CE), who settled on Mt. Lu and did not leave its "Tiger stream" confines for thirty years, there is clear evidence that relatively large groups of wandering monks had settled down by this time and left the life of itinerant mendicants. The independent status of Buddhist monasteries had advanced to an even firmer position. Historically the provincial governors who had come to dwell at Jiangzhou included Huang Yi, Wang Ningzhi, and so forth, all of whom participated at some time or other in Hui Yuan's monastic group activities. Yin Zhongkan, Wang Mi, Liu Yu, Lu Xun, and others, all men with political power, also expressed their respect for Hui Yuan. Throughout the lengthy period of China's feudal society, internal struggles amongst China's political leaders was intense and cruel. The loss of ideals and dashing of all hope were common occurrences. Buddhism created for those who lost the will to continue a world of spiritual stability, as well as a place where one could physically escape hardship and difficulties.

Tao Yuanming's poem *Peach Garden Realm* took a very subjective direction, while the mountain retreats established by Buddhism were physical realities. Once the scholar officials had that kind of retreat, it became for them a relatively purist form of opposition to the internal politics of the ruling class, as well as having an accumulative value for preserving cultural and intellectual life.

Buddhism provided another life line for the ruling class. After the Western Jin, immigrants (i.e., refugees) from the north increased in a manner that the northern kingdoms had little ability to control or solve. Either the refugees stayed behind and risked walking through danger, or fled into hiding places to escape death. Neither alternative was able to preserve a peaceful or settled way of life. The spread of Buddhism brought for these people a way of preserving life and possessions. Many of those fearing increased levies gave their lands to the Buddhist monasteries, as a way of avoiding taxes, and thus inflating the numbers of people living under Buddhist jurisdiction. A new kind of Buddhist monk arose, unlike the intellectuals who relied for their livelihood on contributions from court circles. Since they were not under nationally supported temples and schools, they had to rely on traveling monks who begged for donations, and taxes levied on people living within Buddhist territories, for their means of livelihood. The northern dynasties twice initiated movements to destroy Buddhism, due to the fact that the monasteries had absorbed too many people into their lands, whose taxes were lost to the government, thus affecting the national income. But attempts to destroy Buddhism didn't stop the flow of lay people into Buddhist controlled lands. However, there were limits to the amount of land and the activities of Buddhist in the north. Thus great numbers of people fled south. These groups of people moving southward numbered anywhere from 100 to 1000 per group. They lived in grass huts and caves, foraging for food for ten or more years, and for many more years not having any land to call home (i.e., not recognized as citizens of any kingdom). The great increase and flowering of Chan Buddhism during the Sui-Tang period came for the most part from this source.

Buddhism was a most law abiding and well behaved religion. In its earliest period there were occasional incidents and violent uprisings in the north, but it was not long before the devout followers of Buddhism weeded out the bad elements and carved out small pure and peaceful worlds, free from lawless movements. Monks administered anywhere from 100 to 1000 people who came together to live in close proximity with them. They did not cause trouble, did not revolt, and thus their members it seems developed a sort of natural and mutual trust. Concerning clashes between social groups, Buddhism had a sort of delaying and diffusing function. Zi Pan of the Southern Song Dynasty (North-south Period) told how the monks of his day, whether because their brethren were so many, or the lack of arable land was so acute, from the start used their own physical strength to cultivate vast unused tracts of land from the deep mountains to the shores of the sea. By taking the nation's homeless, and its fallow land, without stealing and usurping that of others, they followed a path that should have been taken by the government. Buddhism was a positive factor in promoting the productive power of society, and opening the southern virgin lands to cultivation.

Commenting on the above, the formation of a Buddhist monastic community added a sort of transcendental quality to feudal society, a third sort of power seemingly opposing the forces that were harmful to the people. It was a social factor of other worldly nature, transcending in appearance any kind of political power or organization, yet that could perform the function of any political power group. Historically it was the greatest preventative force unifying the masses against the concentrated dictatorial powers of feudal government. The only reason why the snares laid against Buddhism (including those set by some Daoist groups) were disarmed by the political authorities was because of the latent political use of Buddhism. It did not seek to form any real force to oppose political authority, nor did it organize any collaboration between politics and religion. Much less did it ever try to organize a group of monks who would actively take part in government. The reason for its success must also be found here.

ZHUANGZI'S THOUGHT
AND THE SPREAD OF BUDDHISM

by Cai Dahua

In coming to China Indian Buddhism, a sort of other worldly cultural thought system, went through a process of understanding and digestion imposed on it by traditional Chinese ways of thinking. In this process the thought of Zhuangzi played a very important role. This influence can be identified not only in the Han and Wei periods (up to 265 CE) when Buddhism first came to China, but is also found in great profusion during the two Qin and the North-South periods (265-581 CE), when Buddhist scholars frequently used the pattern of Zhuangzi's concepts and thought in Buddhist scriptures of similar genre. It is even more important to point out the effect that Zhuangzi's thought had during the golden age of Buddhism, i.e., the Sui-Tang periods (581-906 CE). The Tiantai and Huayan schools' theory of the Meaning of Buddhist Teachings, the Tiantai concept of the various aspects of Dharma Nature, the Huayan doctrines of the "Ten stages of the Dharma realm," and the Chan (Zen) theory of "looking within the heart-mind to understand nature," each received, respectively in its own way and stage of development, the influence of Zhuangzi's thinking on the concept of history, nature, and theory that takes the world and the myriad things as a whole.

I. *The Concept of History: Tiantai and Huayan Stages of Buddhism*

Within the context of traditional Chinese thinking, the concept of history is the point of departure for a lively and spirited form of theoretical discourse. Taking the Confucian way of thought as an example, Zhang Xuecheng says, "The Six Classics are all books of History" (*Wenshi Tungyi*, "*Yijiao*" Chapter). Practically speaking, the essence of Confucianism, when confronted with social, political, theoretical, and moral issues, is to record and sublimate them with the sense of social history. The concept of history in Zhuangzi's way of thinking manifests the process of the origin of the cosmos. Zhuangzi records, "The Great Origin was the *Wu* Transcendent; it had neither material existence or name. It is that from which the One came. The One had material existence, but no form. When material things attained it, they thereby were born; this is called *de*, (i.e., Dao gives birth to De, one, or *Qi* energy/power). It did not yet have form, but (had the power to be) divided (into yang and yin). Then also (in the time-space gap) between the Transcendent and the material there was *ming* life, which flow is called "form." Forms by nature possess *shen* spirit, each with its own appearance, which is called *xing* individual nature. Nature when *xing* perfected by cultivation and practice returns to the state of *de* (undifferentiated form). *De* then can become one with the Great Origin. (See *Zhuangzi,* "*Tiandi*" Ch 12, with the following commentary) *Zhuangzi* calls it:

> Examining into (human) beginnings,
> the origin itself was not gestated;
> not only was it not gestated,
> but the origin also was without form.
> Not only was it without form,
> But the origin was also not *qi* (breath).
> It seethed and glowed in a shapeless expanse;
> Changing, there was *qi* primordial breath.
> Breath changed, and there was form.
> Form changed and there was birth,
> Which until now changes, and there is death.
> (*Zhuangzi*, Ch. 18).

The above passages reflect Zhuangzi's thinking on the process history of nature and life's gestation. Further, Zhuangzi was very strongly influenced by changes in the social conditions of the times... Zhuangzi Portrayed with a some humor another kind of important historical phenomenon -- the history of human vitality and its spirit. In the text of the *Zhuangzi* itself, the Zhuangzi school specifically defined the development of a history of human vitality, seen from a philosophical standpoint, as a process having the following three internal characteristics:

First, it held that the realm of individual human vitality, develops through a historical process from the lowest to the highest point. This is seen in the passage of the *Zhuangzi* where Ru Yu and Nan Puozi Gui are conversing, in the course of which a list of metaphorical sayings occur which describe "learning the Dao" as an unfolding process.

> Yuyu explained the process as follows:[1] "After three days I was able to escape from the changes of nature. Leaving nature's changes, I again followed it (learning the Dao). In seven days I was able to leave aside all things. Once I had left aside things, I again learned from Dao, and on the ninth day I was able to be freed from birthing (life, i.e., the gestation process). Once I had left birthing, I was able to stand before the impenetrable. After audience with the impenetrable I was able to see the absolute (that which is unique, solitary, the `One.') After seeing the absolute, I was able to transcend past and present (there was no past or present). After transcending past and present I could enter into "non death, non birth." Killing the gestation process, there was no death; gestating life, there was no birthing. In such a state of being (i.e., way of existing), there is nothing to be given or taken, destroyed or completed. This state is called *ying ning*, become peaceful by returning to the origin of life; (i.e., running contrary to nature's life and death process leads to *ning* peace). (*Zhuangzi*, Ch. 5).

This passage shows the practice of the Taoist ascetic who by a series of progressive stages passes from a state of being "outside of nature" and "outside of gestation (birthing)" to a condition where there is "no past and present," and "no dying or birthing." By breaking into the depths of what the Taoist spirit pursues as its special quest, we can say that this sort of process bears within it a common pursuit of the human spirit in its highest form, i.e., a progression from the easy to the difficult, from the coarse to the refined, which as it becomes deeper and ever more far reaching in its scope, transcends the self.

Second, it looked on the "Hundred Schools" in its entirety, as a sort of unified albeit complex process that went from a single to many flourishing forms of thought. The Zhuangzi school, in Chapter 33 (*Tianxia*), made for the first time an attempt to organize and put structure into this flourishing and developing school of Pre-Qin thinkers. Chapter 33 taught that the ancient *Dao shu* Taoist arts were everywhere, and that all of these arts were "based on the One." By examining the many branches and threads of Pre-Qin learning, such as Muo Zhai, Qin Guli, Song Xing, Yin Wen, Peng Meng, Tian Pian, Shen Dao, Guan Yin, Lao Dan, and the so many other writers of the school, the *Tianxia* author found that "Each of these writers gained knowledge of one aspect of reality, and is satisfied with it... Each uses their own theory as the norm." Thus their works are but one-sided aspects of the whole.

Third, it was felt that the concrete aspects of Zhuangzi's school and its realm of thought, whether seen as the development of the spirit of individuality or the unifying of the thought of the hundred Schools, was the highest and the latest level of achievement. The Book of *Zhuangzi* explains that his thought had attained the highest realm, "Without north, south, east, or west, its beginnings were in the realms of deep mystery, its returning was to the Great Dao." (N.b., *Datong* here means *Da Dao*; see *Zhuangzi*, Ch. 17). "Above, stroll with the maker of all things; below, be friends only with those beyond life and death, beginning or end." (*Zhuangzi*, Ch. 33). That which best describes the breadth and depth of the core of Zhuangzi's thinking is the passage:

The myriad things are a network, all which must return (to the One)...; it's (outward) order is not exhausted, its coming (back to the origin) is not alone (all must return to it), obscure, hidden, it cannot be used up." (Ch. 33)

Thus Zhuangzi's thought is taken to be the pinnacle of the hundred schools, the end product of the standpoint that develops and expands the human spirit. It is our hypothesis that a major way in which Chinese Buddhism theoretically differs from Indian Buddhism, i.e., the theory of the "Stages of Buddha's Teachings," was developed precisely under the powerful influence of traditional Chinese historiology, of which the influence of Zhuangzi's thought was one of the most important elements.

"The Stages of Buddha's Teachings" is an attempt to analyze and systematize Buddhist scriptures and teachings in historical perspective, as they came into China. In the earlier part of the North-South period (420-580 CE), the Mahayana and Theravada texts were translated and their doctrines spread as they were transmitted from India. However, the differences and contradictions which had developed over many years in the Indian schools of Buddhism, between the Mahayana and Theravada, and within the Mahayana school itself, fascinated Chinese Buddhist scholars from the very beginning. It became an urgent and pressing need to analyze, organize, and explain these Indian Buddhist doctrines that came flowing eastward into China. There were many different theories of dividing Buddha's teachings into stages by Buddhist scholars of the North-south period. Zhiyi's *Fa Hua Xuanyi* (The Profound Meaning of the Lotus Sutra) divided them generically into "Three southern and seven northern" kinds of theories. However, in reality none of these surpassed Hui Guan's (d. 424 CE) earliest theoretical division of the Buddha's teachings into "five periods," and "sudden and gradual" stages of enlightenment. The basis for this theoretical structuring was to take heuristic concepts (such as the phenomenal, non-phenomenal, and permanent), and methods (such as sudden and gradual enlightenment) of the Buddha's teaching as a theoretical way for defining the stages of Buddhist thought and the temporal order of the scriptures. Further, it used the historical analysis of the stages of the Buddha's life, to structure a unified corpus of Buddha's teachings, thus eliminating the seeming contradictions in earlier and later canonical theories.

For instance, the first of the "three southern" theorists was Master Ji of Hu Qiu, who felt that there were three kinds of gradual enlightenment. The Buddha taught 1) various kinds of realist or Sarvastivadin doctrines first, just after his enlightenment. The contents of this teaching belonged to the Theravadin school. 2) Afterwards the Buddha explained the Mahayana Canon, including the Prajna, Vimalakirti, and Lotus Sutras. These favored the teachings of *Sunyata*, the non-reality of phenomena. 3) The last stage of the Buddha's doctrines are found in the Nirvana Sutra, where taking delight in quieting the self, and the doctrine of permanence are explained.

Among the "northern seven" theorists, the Buddhist Master Hui Guang's work *Four Schools* taught that the Buddha's teachings can be divided into 1) co-dependent origination (establishing nature), 2) illusion of name (breaking out of nature), 3) the non true (erroneous phenomenon), and 4) the True (manifesting the real). These divisions included the theories of many canonical sutras, including the Abhidharmakosa, Satyasiddhi, Prajna Paramita, and Nirvana scriptures. Obviously these divisions did not completely coincide with changes that occurred in the historical reality of Buddhism in India. The most important element in the absorption of Buddhist theory (into China) was the infusion of a kind of historical concept unknown in India.

During the Sui-Tang period, with the Tiantai school dividing Buddha's doctrines into "Five stages and eight teachings," and the Huayan school's "Three stages, five teachings," the division of Buddha's doctrines into stages took another step forward. It became clear that the entire corpus of Buddhist learning with all of its characteristics had been swept into a concept borrowed from Chinese history. These theories of dividing Buddhist teachings into stages were similar to the spirit and historical concept of Zhuangzi's thinking in three important ways. First, the Buddhist schools of thought were taken from a single point of origin through an orderly process of development. The Tiantai school held that the Buddha first went through the Huayan (Avatamsaka sutra period), then the *Ahan* (Theravada-Nikaya), *Fangteng* (Vaipulya sutra), Prajna-paramita, and finally the Lotus-Nirvana sutra, five different periods that produced sutras in which the Dharma was explained in different ways.[2] The Huayan school then took this phrase and extended the process of Huayan teaching into three periods: "At dawn, it first shone forth. As the sun climbed in the sky, it continued to shine. As the sun set, it was still shining."[3]

Second, Buddhist scholars' concepts of enlightenment and the Buddha realm followed a step-by-step process of ascent towards full ripening. The Tiantai school (which taught a four stage process towards enightenment) called it the stages of the Triple Storehouse (Tripitaka, i.e., Theravada teaching), i.e., the intermediate, the separate, and the full stages of enlightenment. At the end of the Tang dynasty the Korean monk Diguan used the example of milk, taken from the Nirvana Sutra, to explain this process.

> Those of the two vehicles[4] when sitting at the feet of the Huayan teacher, do not believe or understand, nor do they change their mortal passions; therefore, they can be compared to milk. Next are those who arrive at the Deer Park, where they listen to the Theravada teachings. The people of the first two stages begin to practice Buddhist asceticism. From the vulgar they become sages, and thus can be likened to cream. Next they reach the *Fangteng*, the intermediate stage, where they use Tantric, Mahayana, and Theravada teachings together, and can be compared

to raw butter. Next they reach the Prajna stage, where they respectfully pass on Buddhist doctrines. Their heart-minds are gradually stilled. Now they attain to the separate teaching, and can be likened to warmed butter. Last, they reach the Lotus Sutra; having heard the teachings of all three (vehicles) completely, they attain Buddhahood, and can be compared to clarified butter (gee).
(*Tiantai Sijiao Yi*)

The Huayan school identifies the learning process as follows: the Theravada, beginning Mahayana, final Mahayana, Sudden enlightenment, and the complete teaching. Fazang uses the "real and absolute" theory to explain it as follows:

The little (Theravada) path recognizes the Dharma and negates the self. (It is therefore a non-gate). The beginning (Mahayana) is under the cause of birth, and is the gateway to non-nature. The "final" Mahayana follows both reality and the mind (absolute), a combined way. The "sudden" way of enlightenment brings and end to the use of words, and is the gateway to manifest the absolute. The "full and complete" stage is the Dharma realm, the gateway without obstacle. (*Yuxin Fajie Ji*)

Calming the mind through the use of words (name) is the Theravada way. Calming reason by practice is the beginning Mahayana way. No obstacle between thing and mind is the final Mahayana way. Ending all ties with things to manifest the absolute is the way of sudden enlightenment. The ocean of the Bhutatathata (i.e., the all-containing immaterial nature of the Dharmakaya) universally attained is the way of total completion. (*Huayan Yicheng Jiaoyi Fenji Zhang*, Ch. 2)

Third, each of the schools took their own favorite and most respected canonical text as the highest stage of Buddhist teaching and achievement. The Tiantai school's "Three truths complete merging," (the Madhyamika doctrine of the middle way between affirming and denying reality or the Dharma world) was a teaching which they took to be based on the *Lotus Sutra* (Saddharmapundarika Sutra). They therefore taught that "The Lotus Sutra is the highest Sutra without peer." (Zhiyi, *Fahua Xuanyi*, Ch. 1, *shang*) The following passage is an example of their teaching:

> The ocean has the virtue of the trigram *kan*, (i.e., yin, water). Therefore the myriad streams flow into it. The Lotus Sutra can be likened to it. Just as no river or stream can equal the great ocean in grandeur, so no other canon is as great as it. Thus, the Lotus Sutra is the greatest of all the Sutras.
> (*Fahua Xuanyi*. Ch. 1, *shang*)

The Tiantai school thus considered the other sutras to be like rivers and streams, while the Lotus Sutra was the "Great Ocean."

The Huayan school took as its basic doctrine the theory of "Unlimited Causation," (i.e., the unlimited influence of all things on each other), which was thought to be dependent on the Avatamsaka (Huayan) Sutra. They therefore considered the Huayan doctrines to be the most far reaching and deepest:

> The Avatamsaka Sutra, when spoken penetrates deeper than the ocean, when explained shines on the ruler of the highest mountain. Its wisdom is vast and far-reaching, it exhausts the entire Dharma realm and touches the source of truth. Its wide and subtle words mount to the vast heavens and penetrate each grain of dust in the kingdom.
> (*Huayan Yicheng Jiaoyi Fenji Zhang*, Ch. 1)

They thus set it up as superior to all other sutras, feeling that "The Avatamsaka is a teaching of a different kind of vehicle totally unlike all others." (*Ibid.*) This sort of Buddhist thought, when compared with Zhuangzi's portraying and supporting the process of spiritual stages in "Learning the Dao," shows a certain affinity and similarity with pre-Qin scholars' analyses of scholarship, and respect for respective schools.

Of course, we cannot as yet say that the theories of the Tiantai and Huayan schools' for dividing Buddhist doctrines into periods, and Zhuangzi's concept of a historical process of spirituality were a conscious sort of convergence. But we can conclude definitively that there was a reason why the mapping of a theory for dividing Buddhist doctrines into stages took on a historical outlook within the circles of Buddhist hermeneutics. This ordering was manifest in the classifying of complicated Buddhist sutras and canons into branches and schools, so that the theories and stages had a sense of completeness. Concretely, it is the recognition, from an historical perspective, of a sense of order in a total body of knowledge. The reason for this ordering is found in a sort of power for theoretical creativity, seen in the thinking of Zhuangzi, born from within the very background of Chinese culture itself.

II. *The Concept of an Overall Plan: the Tiantai School's Dharmadhatu and the Huayan School's Dharma World.*

It is an important characteristic of traditional Chinese thought, when compared to Indian Buddhist scholarship, to ponder about a way to arrive at the ultimate source of all things, or to penetrate to the totality that includes all things. During the Sui-Tang period this concept became a part of Buddhist learning. It gave birth to the Tiantai concept of *Xing ju shixiang*, i.e., that the Buddha nature in reality contained all things, good and bad. In fact, this concept was formulated from two other abstract ideas: 1) reality contains all three aspects of the Madhyamika truth (to affirm, deny, and abstain from judging the existence or non-existence of reality, good, or evil), and 2) all the universe is contained in a single thought. One can find the original form of the first mentioned concept, that reality of the Dharma world contains both good and evil, in Indian Buddhist thought. The *Prajnaparamita Sutra* divides the uppermost realm of prajna wisdom into three levels: 1) that possessing the way to the seed of wisdom; 2) that containing the Ekayana (all-in-one) form of wisdom; and 3) that containing the seed of Ekayana wisdom.[5]

The *Dazhidu Lun* holds that these three kinds of wisdom most definitely have a prior and later order, yet can be achieved and held simultaneously at a certain point of accumulation.[6]

>*Question*: "Within one mind every kind of wisdom can be attained, as well as the seeds of every kind of wisdom, by practicing the cutting off of all mental turbulence. The question now is, how to explain the attainment of the seeds of all wisdom after attaining all wisdom, when one must use the seeds of all wisdom to cut off mental turbulence?
>
>*Answer*: Actually everything is attained in a single moment. It is merely explained as a systematic process in order to help people believe in and rely on the Prajnaparamita.

The earliest use of this canonical theory, i.e., "One mind, triple wisdom" to achieve enlightenment by Dhyana (i.e., Chan, or Zen) is found in the writings of the Chan master Huiwen, one of the two founders of Tiantai during the northern Qi period (550-577 CE). It is said that:[7]

>Master Huiwen relied on this text (one mind, triple wisdom) to practice vipasyana in the heart-mind... He contemplated the one heart-mind with triple wisdom, forgetting both, enlightening both, i.e., the path of allowing no thoughts to be born from the very beginning.

He also practiced the "Triple Truth Doctrine":[8]

>All causally produced Dharma (phenomena),
>I say are *sunya* (empty or unreal);
>They are but a false (ephemeral) name;
>They signify in fact the Middle Way.

By taking the idea of *sunya* emptiness to be the "True" Way, the ephemeral or false name to be the popular or vulgar way, and the "center" (judging phenomena to be neither true or false) to be the

Middle Way, and by comparing these to the notion of of "Triple Wisdom, i.e., "All wisdom," "The way to the seed of wisdom," and "The seed of all wisdom," we can see how the concept "One mind, three truths," (One mind, three views) came about. We note how Huiwen's "One mind, three views" impregnated Zhiyi's concept of "The Completion of the Three Ways." It originated from a kind of wisdom that grew out of the *Samatha-Vipasyana* (*Zhiguan*, (i.e., *zhi* the cessation of mind-heart, then *guan* looking outward ability to contemplate phenomena).

However, once arriving at this point where Zhiyi had brought about a kind of change, we find that "the completion of the Triple Way" meant not only a way of contemplating, but also a realm to be contemplated. Zhiyi's disciple Guanding explained this change as follows:

> The Lotus enlightened heart-mind is realm, and Lotus enlightened wisdom is what it contemplates. The realm of contemplation is not dual, it is both illuminated and hidden. That which is called the realm world, is in fact the Three Ways. To know "truth" is an empty contemplation. To know the ordinary is to contemplate the false. To know the center (neither affirm or deny the true or the false), contemplate the Middle Way. The eternal realm has no phenomenon. Eternal wisdom has no cause. No cause is the cause, nothing which is not the Triple Way. No phenomenon, yet real, the Three Ways are complete as a matter of course. (*Tiantai Bajiao Dayi*).

This is also to say that not only do the "Three Ways" embrace all wisdom (eternal wisdom), but they also include all realms (eternal realm). Therefore the Tiantai school's "Completion of the Three Ways" embraces in fact the reality of the entire world (*shixiang*, i.e., concrete reality and its mental appearance). "According to its appearance and nature, it is real, empty, false, and in the middle." (*Fahua Xuanyi*, 2, *Shang*) The doctrine of The Three Ways embrace the concrete and phenomenal aspects of the entire world.

> The entire world in its spatial-temporal aspects, including birthing, growing, karmic deeds, all of phenomena and all that is outside of phenomena, every form and fragrance, there are none of these that are not) in the Middle Way. (*Fahua Xuanyi*, 2, *shang*)

It is obvious that Zhiyi's concept of the "Completion of the Three Ways" underwent a historical and logical process from wisdom, to realm, to original nature. This (process) was quite different from Indian Buddhism's more simple "Empty-false-middle" mode of thought. The "Completion of the Three Ways" (or "Fullness of the Three Truths") in the final analysis took "form and fragrance,[9] all that whereby one maintains life, and the production of karmic deeds," and put all of these into the concept of *shixiang*, the oneness of real and phenomenal. This is again quite different from indian Buddhism, which in the final analysis explained the notion of *shixiang* reality as being *sunya* empty, in the realm of nirvana. It is however very much consistent with the the universalizing concept found in the Zhuangzi, such as "Tao is one with everything," (*Ziwu Lun*) and "The Tao covers and supports the myriad creatures." (*Tiandi*)

Zhiyi's notion of the *Trisahasra* (Three Thousand Worlds, everything in the chiliocosm) found in the phrase "One thought, Three Thousand worlds," was put together from three different Indian Buddhist concepts: 1) the *Shijie* Ten (Dharma) Worlds, 2) *Sanshi* or Triple world, and 3) *Shiru* Ten Essential Qualities of things. The term *Shijie* Ten Dharma Worlds comes from the Lotus Sutra, the notion of the "Six ordinary and four holy" ways of being. I.e., the first six stages of earth and hell are: demon, preta, beast, asura, human, and deva (deity); from heaven are: those who hear the Buddha's voice, those who are awakened to the notion of causality, the Bodhisattva, and the Buddha. All sentient beings are divided among the Ten Dharma Worlds. The divisions are not predetermined, i.e., all sentient beings ascend or descend the stages in accordance with the law of causality. The Ten Worlds themselves are mutually linked to form "A hundred worlds."

The "Triple World" (Sanshi)[10] consists of the realm of all sentient life, the material realm (Guotu), and the psychological realm of mind (Wuyin). This passage, taken from the *Dazhi Du Lun*, relates to categorizing all sentient beings, and dividing them into realms.

As for the *Shiru*, (Ten Essential Qualities), the *Lotus Sutra*, in the "Chapter on *Upaya* Convenient Skillful Means" names the various kinds of Dharma as: the quality of phenomenon, nature, substance, potency, act, source, cause, effect, response, and beginning-end, in sum, the "Ten Essential Qualities" of all sentient beings. This kind of classification organizes all reality into an overall set of generic characteristics. The "Ten Worlds," "Three Realms" and "Ten Essential Qualities" are simultaneously manifest within the "One Heart-mind." By enumerating them, the "Hundred Worlds," "Ten Essential Qualities" and "Three Realms" are the *Trisahasra* (Chiliocosm) 3,000 worlds, which are in turn "One concept, three thousand worlds." Zhiyi stated:

> The One Heart-mind is the Ten Dharma Worlds, and each Dharma World again is Ten Dharma Worlds. Within each of these worlds are thirty kinds of worlds, and thus 100 Dharma Worlds are equal to 3,000 kinds of worlds. These 3,000 worlds are contained in a single thought. If there is no heart-mind, nothing is; if heart-mind is, then there are in fact 3,000 worlds. Thus one cannot say that the heart-mind is prior to the Dharma world, nor can it be said that all the Dharma Worlds came first, then the heart-mind. (*Maha-samatha-vipasyana Sutra Juan* 5)

Thus from the Tiantai school's viewpoint of Buddhist theory, "There is no other Dharma but the *Shixiang* (real-phenomenal) world," i.e., the "3000 Worlds" are nothing other than the reality of the world. Furthermore, they are also the *Shixiang*, the phenomenon that all things possess the same Dharma nature. Examining the concept of the "Three Thousand Worlds" from the standard philosophical perspective, it embodies the underlying presupposition that the entire world exists. From the viewpoint of Chinese thinking, it is quite close to Zhuangzi's statements "The Tao is One" (Ch. 24) and "The Tao is everywhere" (Ch. 22). Within the writings of Zhiyi there are times when in fact he cites the text, or phrases and ideas from the *Zhuangzi*. For instance:

> We must know that we are, and yet are not;
> We do not know, and yet we know....
> Once Zhuang Zhou dreamt he was a butterfly
> Fluttering about happily here and there
> When he awoke he knew he was not a butterfly,
> Or he did not know if reality was a dream?
> (*Maha-samatha-vipasyana*, Juan 5)
> Profound is the origin of the *zhiren*
> (person who has attained the Tao)
> And hard to fathom.
> So much harder is it to define enlightenment
> Sometimes gradual and other times sudden,
> Without definite patterns, its secret traces
> Reaching everywhere, overcoming all obstacles.
> (*Sijiao Yi*, Juan 2)

The passage of Zhuangzi dreaming that he was a butterfly is taken from the *Jiwu Lun* chapter of the *Zhuangzi* (Ch. 2), while the *zhiren* concept (one who has reached union with the Tao) is the ideal kind of person in Zhuangzi's thinking. The fact that Zhiyi cites these passages to explain ideas from Buddhism, proves that the circles of Buddhist scholars who explained the notion of "the Buddha nature includes all phenomenon" were consciously or unconsciously influenced by Zhuangzi's notion of the "Tao," as encompassing the totality of the world.

The content of the Huayan school's theory of "The causal arising of the world" clearly embodied those characteristics of Chinese thought, which organize reality into a systematic totality. It even more clearly manifested the concept of "original nature." The Huayan school's theory of "The Dharma World's arising from conditioned causes" is found in the *Haiyin* ocean symbol of the *Avatamsaka Sutra* (Huayan Jing), a realm of endlessly conditioned causes, which are objectively formed into a cosmic unity, the "Dharma World." Subsequently, it drew from the *Mahayana Sraddhotpada Sastra* (The Mahayana Awakening of Faith) the notion of "having self-inherent existence," and *Bhutatatha* "That which is eternally so" (i.e., that which exists by its very nature). By taking it one step further, it actually changed the unifying principle into "The Dharma World exists by its very nature," and "Single heart-mind Dharma World." The *Mahayana Awakening of Faith* Sastra of course originated from Indian Buddhist sources.[11] But even though the term *Zhenru* Bhutatatha (i.e., the *Zhenxin*, self-existent pure mind) did not change, still the basic dual concept of the "pure and quiet" mind and the *suiyuan* ever changing aspects of mind are a departure from the traditional Indian Buddhist concept.i.e., the absolute mind is unchanging, even though its relation to phenomenal conditions changes. The notion of *Zhenru* has six aspects, according to the *Awakening of Faith* Sastra. It explains the meaning of 'By its own nature' as follows:

> The Bhutatatha by nature is relative... Looking at it from the aspect of 'origin,' by nature it embraces all sorts of meritorious acts.

The term 'acting by its own nature' includes the light of wisdom, enlightening the Dharma world, knowing True reality, the concept of a peaceful heart-mind within one's own nature, the notion of joy within the self, the notion that peace from within the self does not change... these are called the `Tathagata Storehouse.'" (*Rulai zang*) The text also says that the "concept of the ever changing conditioned mind" includes the dual notion of ""violating the self to follow others," and "violating others to follow the self."[12]

The *Mahayana Awakening of Faith Sastra* was written by Asvaghosa, with a commentary attributed to Paramartha. There is no original sanskrit version of this text from India. Indices of texts translated by Paramartha do not carry this title. Critical modern scholarship therefore takes the text to be of dubious origin. Looking at the work from its basic conceptual outlook, the *Mahayana Awakening of Faith* must be subsumed under the genre of traditional Chinese Buddhist thought. Therefore if we take the Huayan School as a typology, in truth the creation of the Awakening of Faith theory was, from its first stages, an assimilation of Indian Buddhist thought into a kind of Chinese Buddhist way of thinking. From the Huayan school's *Haiyin* Ocean Symbol realm of objects it developed the concept of a unified phenomenon (unified origin) from the initial, rather than from the secondary stages of its evolution. The disciples who further elaborated on the Chinese thought concepts of the "Awakening of Faith" were even more distant from (Indian Buddhist) origins.

The Huayan school's formulation of a unified origin to the world, based on the continual arising of conditioned causes from the Ocean Seal object realm, was based on two important, richly creative theoretical ideas: 1) the ten philosophical gateways to no impediment, and 2) the six characteristics of the absolute and the relative.[13] The term "Ten Philosophical Gateways to no impediment" first appears in the *Huayan Yicheng Shixuan Men*, a work of the second Huayan patriarch Yunhua Zhiyan (ca. 640 C.E.). It occurs as a commentary on the translation of the Avatamsaka Sutra in the context of explaining the absolute and conditioned aspects of the myriad phenomena by the phrase "The one is all things, all things are one." Later, the third Huayan patriarch Fazang further developed and perfected the ten gateways, citing the spatial (realms vast and narrow), the temporal (the ten worlds), the quantitative (mutual inclusion of the one and the many), substance and form (sullied things of the world show forth the Dharma), quality (hidden and subtle), relation (main and subsidiary), and other aspects of reality to illustrate the mutual inclusion and shared origin of all things.[14] These are in fact an elucidation of Fazang's statement: "These ten gateways have a single causal rising, the lack of obstacle between the absolute and relative. Although there is only one gate, indeed it leads to all things."

The phrase "The One is everything, all things are one" was one of the original realms of the Buddha, from the Avatamsaka Sutra. But the explanation of the "Ten Gateways" actually brought about a kind of conceptual change, in that the subjective element in the Buddha's "Sea of symbolic images" was changed into an objective cosmic relation, i.e., a cosmic unity. Zhiyan used the *Yin Tuoluo Gang*, the Lotus Mandala (an infinitely multitude of crystals reflecting one another) as an example of the Buddha World, to explain how "The limitless supports the limitless, and though attaining the order of cause and effect, before and after, it neither increases or decreases." (*Huayan Yicheng Shixuanmen*)

Fazang explains: "Of all sentient beings, there is not one which is not in the Tathagata Realm; nor is there one which can enter it." (*Xiu Huayan Aozhi Wangzhong Huanyuan Guan*) It is clear that all of these passages take the Buddhist "Sea of symbolic images" and raise it to a higher level of compatibility with a unified world. The members of the Huayan school consistently took this "One World" as the total Dharma World, or as the "Causal Arising of the Dharma World." Thus Zhiyan states:

> The (Huayan) Sutra says, "That which the tiniest particle of dust manifests is what all of the particles of dust manifest. Therefore the entire nation (earth) is manifest in the smallest particle of dust. Therefore one can take the limitless expanse (of dust particles) to support the limitless

expanse of the cosmos." Such, then, is the arising of the Dharma World. (*Huayan Yicheng Shixuan Men*).

Fazang states:
> The causal arising of the Dharma World, like the net of Indra from which all things come, woven with the pearls of heaven, absolute and relative, identical from within, is boundless, difficult to name. (*Huayan Sanbao Zhang, Xia*)

Dengguan says:
> This Sutra takes the causal arising of the Dharma World ... as its origin. The Dharma World is the unifying of all phenomena, including the ideal and the real, that which is without impediment.... Causal arising is a term for the prime function of substance. (*Da Huayan Jing Liehce*)

The term "Ten Philosophical Gateways to no impediment" first appears in the *Huayan Yicheng Shixuan Men*, a work of the second Huayan patriarch Yunhua Zhiyan (ca. 640 C.E.). The "Six Absolute and Relative Aspects of Reality" are a relative way of looking at phenomena developed by the Huayan school for organizing the Dharma World into a unified cosmos. The proposing and developing of this concept represented the creative aspects of the Huayan school and its thinkers. The "Six absolute and relative aspects of reality," namely: "whole and part, unity and diversity, entirety and fraction," are taken from the *Huayan Jing* (Avatamsaka Sutra), the "*Shidi Pin*" chapter, where it states:

> To vow to do all Bodhisattva deeds, great, vast, limitless, unspoiled, simple, assisting all (sentient beings) to cross over (paramita), to bring peace to all ten Buddha stages, whole and part, united and diverse, entirety and fraction of phenomena, all of the Bodhisattva deeds, these must all be explained in their reality....

This passage is taken from the first of the ten stages of Bodhisattva enlightenment, the fourth vow of the Bodhisattva.[15] Thus the "six phenomena" describe the condition of the heart of the Buddhist in the first stages of practice.

Afterwards Xiqin noted that "each of the ten stages has its own set of six phenomenon." (*Shidi Jing Lun, Juan* 1), i.e., he felt that each of the ten stages of perfection in the *Huayan Jing* comprised the above named "six phenomena." The first stage included the notion of unifying all phenomena, the "entry to the absolute (whole) origin." The remaining nine stages dealt with partial phenomena. Likewise the first stage comprised the "united" and the "entire" while the last nine stages contained the "diverse" and the "harmful" (incomplete) phenomena. This more or less changed the original idea and vastly broadened the scope and content of the "six phenomena" and their use. The members of the Huayan school then took an even greater step, by achieving a leap forward in reasoning: they took the concept of the "six phenomena" which originally were taken to be an attitude of the heart-mind (will and intellect), i.e., an epistemological perspective, and turned it into a way of looking at reality (Fa, dharma), i.e. a principle informing the entire (Dharma) world. Fazang put it thus:

> All of the Dharmas apossess all six phenomena.
> (*Huayan Jing Yihai Baimen*, "*Chabie Xianxian Men*, Ch. 6)
> The causal arising of the Dharma World, the relative and absolute aspects of the Six Phenomena, the simultaneity of Cause and Effect, the independent existence (presence) of phenomena, are a totality of positive and negative flow.
> (*Huayan Yicheng Jiaoyi Fenji Zhang, Juan* 4)

It must be admitted that between the totality of things and the structure beneath them, as between the total cosmos and individual things within it, one can always find a phenomenal relationship between the absolute and relative, sameness and difference, complete and incomplete; it is the presence of this kind of concept within the realm of Chinese thought that is noted. Thus we find in the *Zhuangzi*:

> Tao interpenetrates and makes all things one.
> It's dividing is made whole, its wholeness is dissolved,

> For all things there are neither wholeness or dissolution.
> They again become one in their uniting (with the Tao).
> (*Zhuangzi, Jai Wu Lun*, Ch. 2)

We can conclude from this that the Huayan school's renewing and expanding the idea of the "Six Phenomena" from traditional Indian Buddhism must have been related to Zhuangzi's thinking.

III. *The Concept of Nature and Ch'an Self Nature*

Of the various Buddhist schools during the Sui-Tang period, and throughout the history of all Chinese Buddhism, the school which differed the greatest from traditional Indian Buddhism, and was most deeply imbued with the spirit of Chinese thought was undoubtedly Huineng's branch of Chan Buddhism (i.e., the Southern Chan school of the Tang Dynasty). Chan Buddhism's intrinsic theoretical line of thought was the farthest from traditional Indian Buddhism. As a result of this independence, it had a profound influence and effect. The Chan school's basic theoretical viewpoint was that:

> All Buddhas of the Three Worlds, and the Twelve Scriptures are also within human nature itself, all have the original (Buddha) nature of themselves... One must know one's original heart-mind; in this consists liberation.
> (*The Platform Sutra, Fahai Ben* chapter)

That is to say, the "Buddha Nature" as one's original nature, or "one's own nature" is to be found within each person. Therefore the Chan school's basic religious teaching is that:

> Those who learn the Way to gain instant enlightenment awaken to *Bodhi* perfect wisdom, and attain it from within his/her own original nature.
> (*The Platform Sutra, Fahai Ben* chapter)

It can be admitted that the Chan school's basic theoretical viewpoint and religious direction had their deepest roots in traditional Indian Buddhist scriptures and thought. The four volumes of the Lankavatara Sutra are most important to show this relationship. This text, according to the Chan school, was passed down by Boddhidharma, its founder on Asian soil, to the second Chan patriarch Huike. It was at first thought to be a Sutra used only in China, whereby the benevolent by practicing it could "pass over" from this world (to the shore of enlightenment), as stated in Dao Xuan's *Xu Gaozeng Juan* (see Ch. 1, *Liu Zeng Ko Juan*). Likewise, along with the *Jingang Jing* (Diamond Sutra), it caused Huineng "To be awakened to enlightenment the moment he heard them." (*Platform Sutra, Fahai* chapter)

When examined from a common philosophical perspective, the Lankavatara Sutra's viewpoint that "The Tathagata Storehouse is by its very nature pure and quiescent," provided the Chan school with the concepts "Original heart-mind" and "By its very nature" as basic ontological principles. Thus the statement attributed to Huineng:

> The nature of the ordinary person is pure, like the pure blue sky. But when it associates with the outer world, it is beclouded and covered over with improper thoughts, and its basic (pure) nature cannot shine forth.

(*Platform Sutra, Fahai* chapter)
This actually mirrors the Lankavatara Sutra's version: "The Tathagata Storehouse makes nature pure of itself, but when covered by dust in the world, it is as if one cannot see its purity." This viewpoint is commonly held by the Mahayana tradition. It was divided into twenty-seven categories by Asangha and Vasubandhu, including the entirety of the influential *Diamond Sutra*'s Prajna thought, thus forming the theoretical basis for the Chan school's teaching on sudden enlightenment. Huineng is also credited with saying:

> All those who follow Mahayana, when they listen to the *Diamond Sutra*, their heart-minds are opened and freed for enlightenment. Thus, we know that by their original nature all possess *prajna* wisdom, and of themselves use the light

of wisdom to contemplate, rather than relying on words.
(*Platform Sutra, Fahai ben* chapter)

The *Fabao Ben* chapter of the *Platform Sutra* also describes in a concrete manner how Huineng, when listening to the Fifth Chan patriarch Hungren explain the passage "The heart-mind reponds to nothing and produces no response to phenomena," was suddenly enlightened to the fact that "all of the myriad dharmas are not separate from one's own nature." Therefore, when seen from its source, it is clear that Chan thought does not go beyond the special property and speculative quality of "not using any other than (Buddhist) teachings." Yet when Chan Buddhism stepped put of the theoretical aspects of its origins in Indian Buddhism into the reality of practice in the cultural background of China, it advanced and developed concrete applications which were quite new, i.e., not to be found in Indian Buddhism.

If the theoretical contributions of Chan Buddhism in China can be summarized in a single term, that one phrase would be "self-nature," and the way it was explained and elucidated. Among the Mahayana schools, the term "self-nature" (*svabhava*) occurs frequently, with multiple interpretations. E.g., the four volume *Lankavatara Sutra* says:

> The Tathagata Storehouse is by its very nature still and quiet... At times it is called *sunya* empty, without form (*nirabhasa*), no desire, "Thus," reality, *Dharmata* (Dharma Nature), *Dharmakaya* (Dharma Body), Nirvana, self-nature, that which is neither born nor annihilated, original quiescence, nirvana nature, "Thus is it," etc., all of which are ways of explaining the Tathagata Storehouse.
> (*Lankavatara Sutra, Juan* 1)

The Chan school broke from the fetters of these traditional Buddhist concepts, and used instead a simple form of illumination, quite characteristic of Chinese thought, i.e., it used the cognate concept of *ziran* (nature) to explain *zixing* (self nature) and *benx*-

ing (original nature). An example of this is the work of Shenhui, the first great Chan scholar, who was a disciple of Huineng during his (Huineng's) declining years.[16]

> For the Buddhist monk, the term *ziran* means that all sentient beings have the Buddha nature as original nature. "To have the Buddha Nature and not manifest *ziran*, how is this possible? All of the myriad Dharmas rely on the power of the Buddha nature for their being; therefore all Dharmas are dependent on *ziran*, "that which is of itself." (*A Record of the Sayings of Shenhui [Shenhui Yulu]*)

Besides using the term *ziran* "That which is of itself" to explain self-nature, (zixing), the Chan school also used the expression "original heart-mind" (benxin) to interpret its meaning. Thus one reads in the *Platform Sutra* "To know one's original heart-mind is to see one's own self-nature." Therefore the one central concept that runs through Chan Buddhism from beginning to end is: "Know the heart-mind to see nature, by oneself fulfill the Buddha path;" "To know the original heart-mind and see nature, is to achieve liberation." (*Platform Sutra*, "*Fahai*" chapter)

The Chan school did not go further in developing a clearer explanation of the depth of meaning contained in the terms *ziran* (that which is of itself) and *benxin* (the original heart-mind). However the Chan school does have a story that can be used to further explain this problem:

> Master Snow Peak entered the mountains and broke a stick of wood that looked like a snake. He wrote on it the following words: "No need to carve nature."
> He sent this as a message to his teacher (the Chan Master Da'an). The master replied: "*Bense* (original form) lives in the mountains, unharmed by knife or axe." (*Wudeng Huiyuan, Juan* 4, "The Dharma sayings of Master Bai Zhanghai")

93

Obviously the Chan school's *ziran* "That which is of itself" (i.e., "original nature," "self-nature") refers to a state of natural existence without anything artificial, while *benxin* "Original heart-mind" points to a pristine, natural attitude of mind without any idea. This is why the Chan school explained the notion of "know the original heart mind" -- its basic tenet -- as "no idea is our *zhong* (clan, ancestor), no image is our form, no dwelling is our origin. (*Platform Sutra*, *Fahai* chapter)

The Chan school's concept of *ziran* (that which is of itself), when taken within the context of Chinese traditional thinking, can be said to identify itself with Zhuangzi's views of *ziran* (that which belongs to nature). Thus Chapter Nine of the *Zhuangzi* says:

> The horse stamps its hooves on frost and snow, its hair resists the cold winds, it eats grass and drinks water, it lifts its legs to jump, such is its true nature.
> (*Zhuangzi* Ch. 9)

Thus we can see from the above that Zhuangzi in fact defines the true nature of things from their natural characteristics, (i.e., the true nature of horse is known from its external characteristics, and activities predicated of it, when it acts naturally).

Chan Buddhism's use of traditional Chinese concepts such as *ziran* (nature, that which is of itself) and *benxin* (original heart-mind) to translate and interpret the notions of "Buddha Nature" and "Original Nature" from Indian Buddhism represent a great theoretical change in Chinese Buddhist theory. I.e., it replaces the minute analysis and scholastic elaboration of man's psychological complexities and cognitive process with a holistic, intuitive perception of the original state of man. This theoretical change caused the religious practices of the Chan school to assume a unique form by practicing 1) a totally natural life, and 2) the method of sudden enlightenment of the original heart-mind, the central point or pivot of Chan practice.

1) *The natural way of life.* From the time of the Sixth Patriarch's statement "All the sutras and books exist in nature," and "The twelve kinds of sutras, are all in human nature," (*Platform Sutra, Fahai* chapter) all the subsequent Chan schools held that the "Buddha" realms must all be realized within the "original heart-mind," rather than by seeking enlightenment from studying learned treatises or chanting sutras. Huihai who belonged to the Southern Peak (Nan Yue Heng Shan) branch of Chan said:

> The Buddha is made in the mind. The confused seek him in the written word, while the enlightened find enlightenment in the heart. The befuddled cultivate cause and wait for effect, while the enlightened are awakened in the heart that is without phenomenal form. (*Da Zhu Chan Shi Yu Lu, Juan hsia*).

Xiyun also said:

> Original substance is made in one's own heart; how then can it be attained by seeking it in the written word? (*Huangbi Duanji Chan Shi Chuanxin Fa Yao*).

The Chan school consistently manifested a certain disrespect for Buddhist canonical works in the field of religious practice. Xuanja, the Fourth Patriarch of the *Qingyuan* school (of Chan) stated: "The twelve sections of the Mahayana Canon are but the records of demons and spirits," and shocked the world with:"Gather all of the writings and scrolls into a heap in front of the lecture hall and burn them to ashes." (*Wudeng Huiyan, Juan 7*, "The Dharma Legacy of Chan Master Lung Tan Xin") The Chan School's attitudes towards explaining and practicing the Dharma may sometimes have seemed inappropriate. But from the overall perspective, the Chan school's casting aside of the scriptures was solidly linked to a profound understanding of Buddhist teachings. Such a deep understanding is found in the response of Huihai to the question, "Why shouldn't the sutras be chanted?"

The sutras spread the Buddha's teachings, but do not

attain to the Buddha's meaning... Those who understand the Buddha's meaning are above spoken words. To awaken to the import goes beyond the written word. The Dharma transcends spoken and written word. Why then try to find it (enlightenment) by repeating the sentences over and over? Those who follow the Bodhisattva path attain to the significance and forget the words, are enlightened as to the meaning and leave the teachings, as when one forgets the net having caught the fish, and discards the snare after trapping the rabbit.
(*Sayings of the Chan Master Dazhu, Juan hsia*)

The Chan schools pursuit of the naturally pure *Benxin* "original heart-mind," on the one hand led Chan Buddhists to withdrawal from religious intellectualism, and on the other hand impelled them to consciously go deeper and deeper into spontaneously manifesting the "Original heart-mind" in their daily life. Huihai, when asked the question, "How does one use practice to cultivate the (Dharma) Way?" replied: "When hungry, eat, when sleepy, rest." (Ibid.) Yixuan also said:

Buddhist Dharma is not learned by working hard at cultivation, but by living a simple daily life of non-act. Defecate and urinate regularly, dress and undress, and take nourishment. If tired, lay down and rest. (*A Record of the Sayings of the Linji school's Master Huizhao*)

From the viewpoint of the Chan school, "A simple, unlettered master is worth more than one who has annotated and written commentaries for 100 sutras." (Ibid.) Speaking objectively and impartially, the Chan school took strict and complicated Buddhist religious practices and basically changed them into common everyday life practice. By so doing they did not destroy the spirit of Buddhism in seeking (enlightenment), but rather wanted to embody this spirit in the practice of daily living.

The Chan schools independent nature is expressed thus in the words of Mazu Daoyi:[17]

> The (Buddhist) Way cannot be cultivated. If one says it can be attained through cultivation, the attainment will be lost, just like words spoken and listened to. But if one speak of cultivation, then how is one different from the secular in the street. (*Gujuan Suyu Lu, Juan* 1)

The Chan school's special form of ascetic cultivation (*xiu*) is a kind of "non-cultivation of perfection," an ascetic that is beyond practice and non-practice. It is a spontaneous practice done everywhere and at all times. There is no place which is not a *Daochang*, a place of cultivation.

It is clear that the Chan schools levity towards canonical sutras and attitude of seeking what is natural are easily traced in their origins to traditional Chinese culture as represented in the *Zhuangzi*. Zhuangzi's basic concept of the "Tao" is:

> The Tao cannot be spoken. If spoken it is not the Tao. Know that Tao which bestows form is itself without form. Thus Tao must not be named. (*Zhuangzi*, Ch. 22)

To make such a statement is to say that the underlying principle of the entire cosmos, the formless "Tao" is something that cannot be clearly represented in spoken or written words. Spoken and written words can only give us a sort of analogous idea about the "Tao," but it is not Tao itself. There is a passage in the *Zhuangzi* that explains this point quite clearly:

> A net is for catching fish. It is forgotten, once the fish is caught. A trap is for snaring rabbits. It is forgotten, once the rabbit is snared. Words are meant for the idea. Forget the word, once the idea is grasped.
> (*Zhuangzi*, Ch. 26)

It is again mentioned in Zhuangzi's story of Lunpian, satirizing Duke Xuan, Ruler of Qi, who was reading:

> The ancients died along with their teachings, which they couldn't pass on. Thus what you, my Lord, are studying is but the cast off dregs of the ancients. (Ibid., Ch. 13)

We can see by comparing these passages with the above mentioned attitude of the Chan school to scriptural interpretation, that Zhuangzi's ideas were made a part of Chan Buddhism.

Zhuangzi also favored a form of natural daily living as a way of self-awakening:

> Always follow nature, and do not part from the (Tao of) birthing. (Ch. 5)
>
> Wu-Wei (Transcendent or "No" Act) names my "master."[18] Wuwei plans my *fu* place to reside, Wuwei is my official office, Wuwei knows how to rule me, its substance fills the entire cosmos and is inexhaustible, penetrating to that which is prior to origin. (Ch. 7)
>
> Those (good things) which I store inside me..., are to be responsible for my *xingming* natural life and feelings. (Ch. 8)

and other such passages. The Chan school's "Freedom from cares in everyday life" and other such attitudes towards a natural way of living are similar to the above perceptions of Zhuangzi.

Let us turn again to the second pivot of Chan enlightenment, the special method for sudden illumination of the "original heart-mind." The Chan school held the doctrine that "Buddhahood is created within one's own nature, there is no need to seek it outside the body." (*Platform Sutra*, *Fahai* Chapter). Therefore, the directive to awaken the original heart-mind is a basic religious practice of the Chan school. Since the Chan school did not emphasize literary texts, it did not develop a logical approach to defining the nature of "original heart-mind," or *benxin*. In this way, the awakening of the "original heart-mind" necessarily was produced by a personally felt intuitive experience of the entire physical body -- an "instant enligntenment." This is described by Huineng as, "To suddenly discover that the Tathagata is one's own self-nature." (Ibid.)

The notion of *dunwu* instant enlightenment appears in Chinese Buddhist scholastic thought as early as the Eastern Qin period (317-419 C.E.), in the Nirvana school's writings. The special contribution of the Chan school was the extraordinaray way that it triggered instant enlightenment through *chanji*, the use of words and action. Conundrum words (*gongan* or *Koan*) and physical practice (*dazuo* sitting, blow to the shoulder, etc.) were used to lead on or abruptly cut short and curb the disciple's thinking. The goal of the practices was to enlighten the "original heart-mind." For instance, a disciple asked Huihai, "Who indeed is the Buddha?" Huihai answered: "The one face-to-face with you in the limpid water, if that isn't Buddha, who is it?" (*A record of the Sayings of the Chan Master Dazhu, Juan Xia*)

This is a method of awakening that leads the disciple to enlightenment by looking into a mirror -- or at one's reflection in a lake -- and seeing that in fact I myself am a Buddha. Thus Liangjie's response to a disciple who asked "Who (what) is the Buddha?" was,"Three pounds of flax." (*A Record of Green Jade Cliffs*, *Juan* 2). This kind of response prevents the mind of the questioner from returning to a logical mode, but rather turns the attention to reflecting on one's own physical/intuitive body. These are typical examples of the Chan school's passing on of *Chanji*, i.e., intuitive enlightenment, implicit in questions and answers. The Chan school also used movement to bring about the moment of intuitive enlightenment, as when Daoyi bloodied Huahai's nose (*Gujuan Suyu Lu*), Daoming roughly kicked Wenyan with his foot (*Wudeng Huiyuan, Juan* 15). Because Huaihai and Wenyan were physically hurt, they were enlightened to the fact of "I myself (am Buddha)" and "from this (physical experience) comes enlightenment." The Chan school calls such examples and stories that contain sudden enlightenment, and bring about sudden awakening in the telling *gongan* (Japanese: Koan, conundrum) "Case Records." There are innumerable examples of such *Gongan* in the annals of Chan Buddhism. Some of them relate strange and bizarre happenings, but seen from the perspective of their fundamental goal, all can be comprehended. Perhaps it is due to the distances that occur over time, that some of the concrete historical circumstances in which the *Gongan* were conceived have passed, and disappeared in the mists of bygone ages. This is especially true of those phrases that consider the mind to be an obstacle, and cut off logical thought for "Dhyana awakening." It is because we do not have the historical circumstances of those times as a background that we have difficulty in understanding them in later ages. The original meanings are thus lost.

Besides having lost the historical background for understanding the *Gongan*, the reason why they are so hard to understand also derives from a deficiency in the realm of thought. This lack was not only found in people of later generations, it was also evident in certain Chan monks of that very period. The Chan school's initiating the method of awakening the original heart-mind by sudden *Dhyana* enlightenment, if taken from the standpoint of Indian Buddhism, is a new creation. However, we can find concepts in Zhuangzi that correspond with it. Sudden enlightenment, if we use Huida's explanation, is a totally intuitive grasp and enlightened understanding of an object of cognition that is indivisible. In Zhuangzi's thought, the Tao, which is the ultimate source and organizer of the entire universe, has the same attributes. Thus, Zhuangzi's understanding of the Tao is a sort of holistic intuition. This is then what the *Zhuangzi* says "Look and you will see that the Tao is present in this person; there is no need for word." (*Zhuangzi*, Ch. 21)

To take the Chan saying "Suddenly discover that one's own nature is the Tathagata," as a way of explaining "To understand the mind-heart is to see the (Buddha) nature," is like the *xue Tao* ("learning the Tao") passage of Zhuangzi (see *Zhuangzi*, Ch. 6). In Zhuangzi's thought, the truest and final understanding of the Tao is achieved in the field of spiritual practice, which Zhuangzi calls the *Ti Dao* (to embody the Tao; see Zhuangzi, Ch. 22). The Chan school teaches that "The ordinary heart-mind is the Tao" (*Guzun Suyu Lu, Juan* 13). The process of getting to "know the original heart-mind of oneself," is an experience that is a part of daily life.

> To follow the law of causation and eliminate past karmic deeds, just follow nature in wearing clothes.

(*A Record of the Sayings of Linji Master Huizhao*)

This also corresponds to Zhuangzi's "embodying the Tao." One can see that although the Chan school's "awakening to original heart-mind" is quite special, still, it is structured on two basic methodological factors: 1) holistic intuition, and 2) practical experience, the source of which is found in the *Zhuangzi*, a part of traditional Chinese culture.

It must be said that Chinese Buddhist studies changed from the original theoretical path of Indian Buddhism to a kind of thought that was characteristic of China, and which developed independently. It was a particularly difficult transformation, ...far more complicated than we were able to express above. In this article we simplified the explanation, dividing it into three theoretical aspects, that is, the historical, general, and natural. This was done to show that Chinese Buddhism departed from Indian Buddhism, and was dependent upon Chinese perennial philosophy. In this process, Zhuangzi's thought fulfilled an important role.

THE THEORY OF BUDDHIST SPIRITUAL REALMS AND CHINESE ART IMAGERY

by Jiang Shuzhuo

In Buddhist theory, the Buddha Nature, that potential which every person has by nature for enlightenment, comprises both the mind and imagination, i.e., the realm of mind and the objective realm. Furthermore, in the *Maha Parinirvana Sutra* the Buddha Nature (*fuoxing*) at first was translated as *Fuojie*, the Buddha Realm. Zhu Daosheng (360 - 434 CE) of the Southern Kingdoms, in explaining the Buddha Nature, held that the Buddha Realm was the most fundamental concept.[1] We can see from this that the theory of the Buddha Realm has a very close relationship with the theory of the Buddha Nature.

During the two Jin and the North-South periods the theory of the Buddha Nature flourished in an unprecedented manner. The word *Jingjie*(Realm) appeared frequently in Chinese translations of Buddhist scriptures. For instance Buddhabhadra's translation of the *Avatamsaka Sutra* (*Huayan Jing*) during the Eastern Jin period, Kumarajiva's Qin translation of the *Fajie Tixing Jing* during the later Qin, Bodhiruci's translations of the *Lankavatara Sutra* (*Rulanka Jing*), the *Sukhavativyuha Sutra* (*Wuliang Shou Jing Lun*), Dharmaruci's translation of the *Rulai Zhuangyan Zhihui Guangming Ru Yiqie Fuojing Jie Jing* (The Tathagata Splendid Wusdom Light Enters the Entire Buddha Realm Sutra), the Liang Dynasty monk Jiapuoluo's translation of the *Du Yiqie Zhufuo Jingjie Zhiyan Jing* (a different translation from Dharmaruci's), Paramartha's translation of the *Zhongbian Fenbie Lun*, the *Yogacara Sastra*, *Mahayana Sraddhotpada Sastra* (*Dacheng Qixin Lun*), *Shiba Kong Lun*, and so forth, all contain the expressions *jingjie*, *Fajie*, and *jing* and other such terms. During the Tang dynasty, the translation of the Faxiang school's Great Master Xuanzang, *Yogacaryabhumi Sastra* (*Yujia Shidi Lun*) (a work of

Asanga), the *Vidya-Matrasiddhi Sastra* (*Cheng Weishi Lun*) the *Zaji Lun*, the *Maha-Vibhasa Sastra*, (*Da Piposha Lun*), the *Abhidharma-kosa Sastra* (*Jushe Lun*), the terms occur frequently. Discussions of the Buddha World (Jingjiei) and the Dharma World was fashionable in the Huayan, Sanlun, Chan, and other schools. Under such an intellectual atmosphere, with the custom to revere the Buddha image, the world of Buddhist theory gradually penetrated the realm of aesthetics.

Beginning with the *Poetics* of Wang Changling (698-757 CE), and the Monk-poet Jiao Ran's *Poetic Form*, the notion of a Buddhist realm was used to explain the relationships between the objective and subjective. From this concept the notion of an artistic realm was born. From then on, the notion of a Buddhist realm enriched the aesthetic world.

I

The basic doctrine of Buddhism is the emphasis placed on co-dependent origination in the universe, and mutual causal relationship. The *Agamas* (the Nikaya documents of early Buddhism, Vols. I and II of the Taisho Buddhist Canon) says:
> This is born, therefore that is born;
> This annihilated, therefore that is annihilated.
> This exists, therefore that exists.
> This is not, therefore that is not.

This kind of theory of conditioned arising is the basic cognitive method of Buddhism to observe, know, and understand the cosmos.

Depending on the Buddhist way of viewing the theory of conditioned arising, none of the Buddha realms are separate from cognition. Everything in the world is the product of the mind's knowing. There are eight kinds of consciousness: that which comes from the eyes, ears, nose, taste, touch, intellect, *mana* (active mind), and *alaya* (seeds of consciousness). Each of these eight modes of consciousness are born of themselves, and are accompanied by a corresponding mental response. From this, they can be distinguished from other phenomenal realms. E.g., vision is born from the core of the eye, and recognizes color. The hearing is born from the core of the ear, and recognizes sound. The sense of smell is born from the core of the nose, and recognizes odors. The sense of taste is born from the root of the tongue, and recognizes flavors. The sense of touch is born from the entire body, and recognizes the light and the heavy, cold and warm, smooth and rough. The intellect is born from the core of the mind, and it recognizes the entire Dharma world (Dharma includes everything in the mental and real world). The *Mana* (active mind) is born from the *Alaya* (seed of consciousness mind). It recognizes the illusion of self and takes it to be (its own) realm. Speculating from this knowledge, it ascends to the realm of intellection (the measure of thought). The Alaya consciousness uses the Mana as the source of its arising. In recognizing the seeds, the root, and the vessel as the realm of phenomenal reality, it contains the seeds of the entire Dharma world, which are contained on the seventh sense (Mana), the storehouse of consciousness. The prior six roots and forms of consciousness basically refer to the corresonding functions of the sensory system. The last two add the element of reasoning. Because of this, that which Buddhism calls the "Buddha World," is the mutual relationship between the mind and its object, (i.e., the mind, and its reflections as objects of knowledge).

    Ding Fubao, in translating the term *jing* (realm), said:[2]

    Where the mind wanders, and becomes entwined, is realm. For example, color is where the vision dwells, and thus is called the realm of color. As for the Dharma world, that is where consciousness reaches.

    According to this explanation, realm is the object of mind's cognition. Only when mind is entwined (occupied), is there realm. To explain the word *jie* world, aside from its meaning, to distinguish and explain the kinds and nature of things, it also has the meaning of *yin* cause. Cause is the "reason why another thing arises (is born)." Citing the *Bai Fa Shu* (Book of 100 Dharmas):[3]

> "World" means "Cause." Within it their are six concepts, arising from six roots, and born from six reals. That which is knowledge, that which is cause, is called *jie* world.

This notion of world is different from the traditional Chinese sense. It points to the cause, source, and condition.

In summation, there are three main views in the Buddhist theory of the relationship between sensation and realm. 1) Knowledge is born from the phenomenal realm. The ability to see, hear, smell, taste, and even to analyze cannot be separated from the material phenomenal world of color, sound, fragrance, flavor, and touch. I.e., their appearance is rooted in and conditioned by the phenomenal world of color, sound, fragrance, flavor, and touch.

2) Apart from consciousness there is no phenomenal world. I.e., all of the external, objective world is gestated by the mind. As said in the *Great Awakening of Faith*:

> Everything is Dharma; only according to the mind is there distinction. If there is no human mind, there will be no phenomenal world. The three worlds are empty. They are the product of the mind. There is no world of dust (six sensations), without mind.

The above two points explain the co-dependent relationship between cause and effect. Mind is potential cause, and the phenomenal world is actual cause. There cannot be one without the other, i.e., they canot be separated. This is the origin of the later Chan saying: "Dharma is not an orphan birth; it is born with the objective world." According to the Buddhists,[4]

> Root, cognition, and realm, the three Dharma, are interdependent. Cognition is born together with root and realm, rather than being born from them. All phenomena rely on each other as cause.

3) The mind can wait upon, gather from, and change "realm," and not simply reflect objective phenomena. This point mainly explains the dynamics of Buddhist psychological activity. E.g., psychological activity produces concept, which actively waits upon and draws from realm. When root and realm are connected with each other, the intellect itself has a kind of power which leads the mind and the object of mind to simultaneously touch the same realm. It gives birth to sensation, that is, touch (*sparsa*). After touching *realm*, there is a certain feeling and impression left on the mind. This is called *shou* (vedana) the act of sensing a thing. On such a foundation, sense will experience a sudden change, i.e., it will be able to analyze and judge, the act of thinking. After thinking, the intellect is still able to have its own way of disposing of the phenomenal world, that is speculation. From idea to speculation is a gradual process from sensation to reason, in which the intellect plays an active role of advance and change (from sense to reason). Thus in Buddhist epistemology there is notion that "realm" is changed by the mind. This includes integrating dialectical relationships between realm and mind. Emphasis is placed on the dynamics of mind as subject.

As for the contents of *realm*, there are three kinds: 1) *the realm of nature* (*xing*), i.e., general material phenomena, e.g., color, sound, fragrance, flavor, and touch. All of these are the realm of actuality. Direct reasoning (*xianliang, pratyaksa*) comes from the realm of nature. Direct reasoning refers to mind as potential cause, and realm as actuated cause. These two are simultaneosuly present, with no intermediary, e.g., as eye to color, ear to sound, all of these are examples of direct reasoning.[5]

> It refers to pure sense knowledge, in precise terms, a direct mode of reasoning, a knowledge gained by intuitive powers that leaves discrimination, and, still orderly, follows the reality of externally existing phenomena.

2) *The Realm of Illusion* (*Duying Jing*), which includes two kinds: i) the realm of substantial illusion. Though they have real existence, they are not physically present, but are caused by the influence of the mind which imagines them present. This in fact is a kind of random memory. ii) The realm of non-substantial illusion. There is no such realm, but it is solely caused by the illusion of the mind hypothesizing its existence. An example of this would be a furry turtle, or a horned rabbit. This is a kind of illusion, a kind of imagined phenomenal world. From the realm of substantial illusion is born the power of comparison and inference. Inference is "the intellectual power to recognize things by comparing differences and following commonplace similarities (by comparison and contrast).[6] That is, inference postulates some thing or principle according to random memory or an imagined world of phenomena, from the angle of common sense knowledge.

3) *The Realm of Matter*, which also contains two kinds: i) the realm of true matter, such as using the mind to cause mind. The phenomenal world held by the mind is true and not empty. ii) The Realm of Apparent Matter, such as using the mind to cause color. It sees things with the color blue, yellow, red, or white, but since there is no real material thing which bears this quality, the name of the thing is false. The concept of non-discrimination arises according to the realm of matter. Though this reasoning seems to be direct, in fact it is not truly direct. It seems to be inferring, but is not truly inferring. In fact this reasoning is a kind of specious illusion and false tenet. Thus it is called non-discrimination, e.g., "mistaking the reflection of a bow in a cup for a snake." Seeing the three realms together, the term "realm" in Buddhism includes the objective external realm as well as the internal subjective realm of man. Buddhism takes all material and spiritual phenomena as *jing* realm.

The theory and style of thought of the Buddhist Realm had a great influence on the aesthetic scholars of ancient times, who defined the content and discussed structure of the realm of art.

The first sprouts of the theory of the "Thought Realm" could be traced back to the *Yizhuan* (Commentaries on the Book of Changes) of the pre-Qin period, and the Neo-Taoist debate on the meaning of words, during the Six Dynasties (222-589 CE). They provided a manner of discussing the "theory of the thought realm" from the epistemological viewpoint. That is to say, looking at objects, an image is formed. When a mental concept is formed, the image is forgotten. When the image is received, the word is forgotten. Thus Zong Bing says, in his *Introduction to Shanshui (Scenic) Painting*, "Hold onto the Tao to respond to things," and "Clear the mind to taste images." Liu Xie states "Spirits wander with things," (from the *Wenxin Diaolong*, the *Shensi* chapter), and Yao Zui says "Be rooted in the myriad images, embrace them in the heart."(*Xu Hua Pin*). In these theories they meant to probe the unification of things and mind in the creation of art. Although they did not directly adopt the concepts and terms of "Realm," or "the Buddha Realm," which had already appeared in Buddhist circles of the time, still they paved the way for the theory of the "Buddha Realm" of the Tang dynasty.

Looked at from the viewpoint of internalizing the development of aesthetics, the Tang dynasty theory of the Buddha Realm is the product of a deepening level of discussion of the unification of mind and things. Following the flourishing of the arts and literature during the Tang dynasty, it is totally natural that there would be a new general summary and refinement of the theory (of aesthetics). Using the theory of the Buddha Realm to illustrate the theory of realm in art, is directly related to the social circumstances and atmosphere of the time, as well as the recognition by Chinese artists of a mode of thinking coming from Indian Buddhism.

The first discussion of "Realm" in Tang Dynasty poetry appeared in Wang Changling's *Poetic Style (Shige)*[7]

In his *Poetic Style* Wang Changling says:

To write poetry, one must focus the mind. Once the eyes

touch things, the mind goes with them, and enters deeply into this realm. It is like climbing to the top of a mountain and looking down on the myriad things below. It seems as if everything is in the palm of the hand. Seeing so many things in this manner, the heart-mind perceives clearly. At this moment one can begin (to write poetry).

The "Realm" discussed here refers to objective phenomena as seen through the eyes of the artist. Wang Changling held that to write a poem, the poet should touch things with his mind, and understand in depth the myriad things as objective phenomena. Here he uses dynamic words such as "touch" and "penetrate," intending to emphasize the power of the poetic mind to enter into objective phenomena. This is related to the birth and formation of the realm of thought. He explains that the thought realm is the result of the mutual penetration of the subjective aesthetic judgement and its object, (i.e., objective phenomena).

Wang Changling says in another place:

> The pulse and luster of the four seasons gives birth to ideas in accord with the moment... Once the eye sees the thing, and takes it into the mind, the mind enters the thing, and the thing enters the word.

This was a step forward in illustrating the relationship between mind and things, after the *Wuse* chapter in Liu Xie's *Wenxin Diaolong*. The two words "enter" precisely explain the corresponding relationship between the mind and the thing. Here the entering ot the thing into the mind, and the mind into the thing, is another way of explaining Liu Xie's:

> Depicting the atmosphere and scenery
> Follows the meandering of nature;
> Color and sound wander with the heart-mind.

This is also consistent with his saying, "Touch the thing with the mind, and enter deeply into their realm" (ibid).

Wang Changling also discussed the relationship between emotions in the artistic blueprint of the poem and realm:

To write an essay is to express ideas... If the thought doesn't come, open the emotions and lose the mind. Let the realm give birth to itself. When one lets the "realm" reflect it, then thought comes. The essay comes with the thought. If thought and the realm do not unite, one can't begin to write.

Here "Realm" no longer refers to objective phenomena. Rather, it is the realm of the poet's mind, or a mental phenomenon, when he formulates the blueprint. The realm of the poet's mind has the function of activating and initiating the poet's artistic blueprint. If the poet is bogged down, he/she should let go of the mind and arouse various kinds of phenoma in the memory, and thus awaken poetic emotions. The above quotation is also a discussion of the coordinating relationship between the artist's emotions and the objective phenomena of artistic creation.

Wang Changling's use of the term realm here, has the meaning of *Duying jing*, "Non-substantial imagination" in Buddhism. This points to a kind of superficial image in memory and an illusion of the mind. Quite the opposite of objective phenomena, the realm in the artist's mind is not a true image of the external. Rather it is a mental picture that has been worked on by the artist.

If one says that Wang Changling's theory of realm borrows the Buddhist theory without being aware of it, then when we come to the well known monk Jiao Ran of the Jiangdong regions (Zhejiang and parts of Jiangsu and Fujian), we see that he consciously applied the theory and terms of the Buddha Realm to illustrate the poetic realm. In his poetry and poetic theory he said:

When entering the realm, one won't find the the most brilliant expression, until tasting difficulty and danger. (*Shishi*, *Qujing* chapter)

When a poet's thought begins, the higher the realm, the higher the content of the entire poem; the lower (looser)

the realm, the lower the content.
(*Shishi, Biantiyou Shijiuzi*)

When the realm (of imagination) itself is endless, then comes the emotions. (Ibid.)

The poetic emotions derive from the realm, the Dharma Nature is found in emptiness. (*A Poetic Response to the Official Lu's Discussion of the Meaning of Nirvana....*)

Not until you try, will you know how hard it is to build a realm; to forget the image and meet the spirit is not on the tip of a brush. (*In Honor of Official Yan, Xuanzhenzi, at the Zhenqing Taoist Temple, provided a feast, music, dance, and painted the Dongting Sanshan Ge*).

Obviously the terms used here, such as "capturing the realm," "following the realm," and "building the realm," are borrowed from Buddhist scriptures. But, Jiao Ran did not blindly use Buddhist terms. Rather, he absorbed the corresponding theories from them, worked them over, and made a general summary of the creative aesthetic process. In discussing the creation of the thought realm, Zhao Ran went a step further than Wang Changling. Wang Changling held that the fusion of mind and realm was the primary way to create the thought realm. Jiao Ran did not only explain the abstract truth that "poetic emotion derives from realm," but also suggested an aesthetic standard: "when the realm itself is endless, then comes the emotions." He held that the birth and growth of the thought realm is the fusion of the poet's emotions and "realm of imagination." The poet must dedicate his emotions to capture the objective realm. To measure the level of the poetic realm, one has to let the emotions reach the realm of endless imagination, and whether or not its artistic beauty has a "lasting after taste." Jiao Ran's point of view marks the first formulation of the theory of thought realm. It also provided the earliest theoretical mode for later scholars of aesthetics, furnishing the idea that the thought realm is the integration and unification of emotion (qing) and material background (jing). After Jiao Ran when scholars discussed the birth and growth of the thought realm, they basically followed this theoretical mode to supplement, elaborate, and perfect aesthetic theory.

Si Kongtu of the Late Tang period proposed that "thought is in harmony with the realm of imagination," (*Yu Wang Jia Ping Shi Shu*), emphasizing the mutual agreement between emotional thought and the material realm of imagination, in the process of artistic creation. During the Song Dynasty, in his discussion of poetry, Jiang Kui held that "In mind is material background, and in material background there is mind." (*Baishi Daren Shi Shuo*) Zhang Yan proposed "the forging of emotion and background," (*Shiyuan, Liqing* chapter). Ye Mengde required that "thought meets the realm of imagination," (*Shilin Shihua*). Fan Shiwen held that "Emotion and background are mutually fused and inseparable," and "Setting without emotion does not bloom; emotion without background does not beget," (*Dui Chuang Ye Yu*).

There were more sayings similar to these during the Ming Dynasty. For example, "The sense of a poem is found in emotion and background. Neither can be achieved standing alone, nor are they mutually exclusive." "The background is the medium, and (emotion is) the foetus; together they make a poem." "Emotions and background embrace each other and become a poem." (Xie Zhen, *Siming Shihua*). "The body and external things are connected, and give birth to the realm of imagination; the realm of imagination and the body are connected, and give birth to emotion." (Zhu Yunming, *Sung Cai Zihua Huan Guanzhong Xu*). "The mixture of emotion and background." (Hu Yinglin, *Shisou*). "Spirit and background are joined," "Feelings are in harmony with background," (Wang Shizhen, *Yiyuan Zhiyan*). "Interpenetration of mind and background," (Zhu Cunjue, *Cun Yutang Shi Hua*), etc. All of the above authors believe that the structure of the realm of imagination is the active integration and unification of 1) the mind and the thing, 2) emotion and background, and 3) spirit and realm.

With regard to this point, Qing dynasty scholars had an even clearer idea. Bu Yantu, a painter of the early Qing Period proposed in a succinct way "Emotion and background are the realm." (*Huaxue Xinfa Wenda*). This is a most distinct and direct explanation of the structure of "realm." Wang Fuzhi's discussion about the relationship between emotion and background is the most complete. It could be said that it reached the peak.

He felt that 1) "the emotions and background, though apparently dichotomous, are in fact inseparable." "Setting is fulfilled by emotions, and emotions are born from the setting. They are not separate from the very beginning, and it was the idea that brought them to fruition. Once they are separated, the emotions are not enough to express feeling, and the background is no longer the background." (*Jiang Zhai*, Vol. II). Therefore, in artistic creation, once "the emotions and the setting are integrated, good expression comes naturally." If the view alone is described, then there is no view." (*Ming Shi Pingxuan*, Vol. 5). In the most excellent artistic works, there must be "emotions that arise from the setting, and settings contained in the emotions." (*Tang Shi Pingxuan*, Vol. 4).

2) He suggested that the emotions and settings could be inclusive, mutually enhancing, gestating, and prevailing on each other. He said, "Even though the emotions and the settings distinguish between mind and thing, still the setting gives birth to the emotions, and the emotions produce the setting, the touch of sadness and happiness, honor and shame, dwell within each other." (*Jiang Zhai Shi Hua*, Vol. 1). "Emotions are not empty; they can always be put into a setting. The setting is not sterile, and always conceives emotions." (*Gushi Pingxuan*, Vol. 5).

These ideas of Wang Fuzhi, compared with his predecessors, are more mature. They explain more precisely the co-dependent relationship between emotions and realm in the process of artistic creation. In its spiritual aspect, it fits the Buddhist idea of co-dependant origination. After Wang Fuzhi, the well-known scholar Wang Guowei of certain achievements in Buddhism, went a step farther in clearly explaining that:

> The realm is not an isolated setting. It also includes moods of happiness, joy, anger, and sadness. Thus, those who can describe real settings and real emotions are those who can describe realm. Otherwise, it is not a realm. (*Renjian Cihua Fulu*).

This manner of speaking is obviously a transplant and extension of the theory of the Buddha Realm. Wang holds that the realm does not only include the objective setting, but also includes the interior realm of the poet himself. This makes the two connotations of "realm" held by his predecessors even more clear. In his book *Wenxue Xiaoyan* (A Brief Commentary on Literature), he also pointed out that there are "Two original matters in literature, setting and emotion." He again said:

> Internally, literature expresses the inner self of the writer; externally, it moves the reader. This is because of both idea and realm. What has been said means that idea and realm are combined. Either realm overpowers, or the idea overwhelms. If one or the other is missing, there will be no literature. (*Wenxue Xiaoyan*)

He regards the integration of idea and realm, settings and emotion, as the internal characteristic of good literature. Wang Guowei's theory brings the classic theory of realm to completion.

What must be noted is that when aesthetic scholars of the Qing Dynasty discussed the birth of realm, they especially emphasized the function of objective settings. For example, Cheng Zhe said in his *Yuyang Xu Shixu*:

> The way of poetry originates from the emotions;
> i.e., it is born from setting.

Wu Qiao also said, "The emotions do not arise by themselves, but rather from the setting." (*Wei Lu Shihua*, Vol. I) Wang Fuzhi applied the Buddhist theory of realm to his idea of "The setting being one with mind," which is measured by *Pratyaksa* (immediate insight). He used this to emphasize the importance of "obtaining the setting and the (poetic) phrase from what is grasped by the mind's eye." (*Tang Shi Pingxuan*, Vol. III) He said:

> That which the body experiences, and that which the eyes see, are the limits... The phrase "The monk knocks on the gate under the moon," is from the imagination, as if he is narrating the dream of another. Even though he gives a vivid description, the heart isn't really touched.
>
> Those who think this is the right way, follow the poet's concern about choosing between the two words "push" and "knock." If they unite setting and mind, then there must be only one choice between "push" and "knock." It would have come naturally, according to the setting and feeling. What need is there to worry about it? There is no fixed setting in the phrase "Round sun sets over the long river." "Ask the boatman on the other side of the river," is not something that can be composed only in the mind. This is the Chan Master's "immediate insight" (*Pratyaksa*).
>
> (*Jiangzhai Shihua*, Vol. II)

Wang Fuzhi's use of the concept *Pratyaksa* is not a far-fetched or irrelevant analogy. He truly showed something in common between the two (setting and feeling). Professor Zhang Wenxun once said, "Wang Fuzhi's analogy is in accord with the three elements of *Pratyaksa*, i.e, its phenomenal, real, and intuitive nature, emphasizing the need to use the phenomenal, reality, and intuition in creating the poetic experience. In Chapter III of his book *Xiangzong Luosuo* he explained the concept *Pratyaksa* (xianliang):

> Xian has the meaning of "presence," and "ready made." It has the idea of "let truth manifest itself." The present does not have a shadow in the past. Ready made feeling, once touched, responds immediately. There is no room for thinking about it. The appearance of the objective

leaves no doubt about its existence. There is nothing phony about it.

The Tang poet Wang Wei's (701-761 CE) phrase:
>The smoke rises straight over desert sands,
>The round sun sets over the long river.

is also the product of this "one touch response." It gives the reader a clear and direct picture. Also, similar phrases such as "Spring grass grows in the pond," "Butterflies flutter in the southern garden," "Bright moon shines on snow," are "the amalgam of mind and eye, which when they come forth as words, are like round pearls and limpid jade. What each one holds must be seen on its own terms, along with how it fits into the setting." (*Jiang Zhai Shihua*, Vol. II) This is also an evaluation based on the idea of immediate insight (*Pratyaksa*). Concerning the critique of Ruan Zi's poem *Yonghuai*, found in the *Gushi Pingxuan*, Vol. IV, Wang Fuji in disussing the phrase "Early comes the cold breath of Autumn," says:

>The "true storehouse of sight perception" for the poet is to use the pen of "following light and capturing setting, to express the feeling of touching heaven and penetrating the heart."

The "true storehouse of sight perception," is a Buddhist term for what the Buddha called the "highest true Dharma." The Chan masters regarded it as the "Buddha mind" (i.e., the *xinyin* "seal of the heart-mind") passed on by secular transmission. Wang Fuzhi borrowed it to refer to the basic principle or methodology of poetic creation. He meant to emphasize the integration of eye and mind, emotion and setting.

Wang Fuzhi introduced the Buddhist theory of *Pratyaksa* to illustrate the creation of realm, and to bring to it a more speculative color. After this, Wang Guowei suggested the theory of inseparability, which is similar to Wang Fuzhi's theory of immediate insight. In Wang Guowei's usage, the word "separability," means the lack of phenomenal, real, and intuitive nature. He took phrases such as "After dusk, the many hills speak of isolation," and "The evening cicada, in the high trees, chat about news of the west wind," to show that they are like "Flowers in the fog, i.e., there is always a layer in between." (*Renjian Cihua*) That is to say, it does not connect directly to their true nature. "Inseparability" is found in poetry where:

> Each word brings before the eyes a vivid picture... The description of the setting is refreshing to the reader's ears and eyes. The words come out naturally, without a hint of artificiality. (*Renjian Cihua*)

This kind of poetry with its artistic images, makes the reader experience intense intuitive feelings. For example Xie Lingyun's phrase "Spring grass grows in the pond," Ouyang Xiu's "Clouds and lake embrace at the horizon," and so forth. This kind of inseparability is what *Pratyaksa* requires. The conditioning and the conditioned, with both present at once, have no "word" or "specific name" separating them. Rather it is pure sensory knowledge, again born from the nature of the thing itself.

From Wang Changling to Wang Fuzhi and Wang Guowei, the theory of realm advanced gradually from rudimentary formation to maturation and perfection. During this time, the discussion about the contents and the structure of "realm" went through a step-by-step process of clarification and completion. The absorption of Buddhist theory is also a process of recognition, digestion, transformation, and conversion. We could almost say that Wang Changling and Chao Ran directly accepted the theory of the Buddha Realm, and utilized the idea to propose a theory of aesthetics.

During the Ming and Qing Dynasties, the theory of the Buddha Realm was digested, revised, and transformed. Take Wang Fuzhi for example. His holistic philosophical system is materialistic. But this did not prevent him from absorbing the notion, terms, and style of thinking of Buddhism to enrich his materialistic philosophy of aesthetics. Although he used the Buddhist concept of *Pratyaksa* (Immediate insight), he underscored the important function that real life has in artistic creation. Again using Wang Guowei as an example, when he defined the content and structural elements of realm, he applied the theories and style of Buddhist thought, though on the surface one could barely see any religious connection.

II

As mentioned above, Buddhism calls all material and spiritual phenomena "realm." According to Buddhist epistemology, neither the objective external world, nor the internal world actually exists. The "realm" originally does not have existence. Only because of the ability of the mind to conceptualize, is there a corresponding conceptualized phenomenal realm. The conceptualized phenomenal realm is apparently an actual realm, but in fact is not. Reality and thought are distinct; thus the Buddhist concept that there is only thought, and no (real) realm. Still, the "non" realm is not an absolute void. It is a realm apart from cognition. It is an apparent realm that is not recognized, but self changing. The *Cheng Weishi Lun* (Vidya-matra Siddhi Sastra) Vol. I says:

> The external realm manifests itself according to feelings Thus, cognition does not exist of itself. Therefore internal cognition must arise from co-dependent origination. Thus, realm does not non-exist.

This is the Buddhist concept of "Internal existence, external void." Furthermore, even though all of the phenomenal worlds differ in appearance, they do not have actual substance of themselves, like dreams and blowing bubbles, flowers in a mirror and the moon in a river. They can be seen, but have no substance to be grasped. It is just as the *Maha-Vibhasa Sastra* says:

> Realm, has color (rupa) and no color,
> Can be seen and not seen,

> Has an object, and no object,
> Acts, and does not act,
> Responds and has no response,
> Depends on something, and depends on nothing,
> Is caused, and has no cause,
> Has form, and no form.

Thus, the Buddha Realm is a kind of world that neither exists nor non-exists. In addition, from the viewpoint of co-dependent origination, all sorts of things arise and are annihilated according to causation. This is easily misunderstood as meaning that there is real substance and annihilation. In fact,[8]

> The root meaning of co-dependent origination is that there is no real substance or annihilation. This will not be clear, until one does away with the misunderstanding that arising and annihilation are real.

The Madhyamika school's explanation of co-dependent origination holds that arising and annihilation are not real, but only seeming. In fact, the corerect way to put it is: Non-arising and non-annihilation. The *Prajna Paramita Sutra* says:

> All dharma are by nature empty. There is no arising and no annihilation. When causes coincide, there is arising. When causes separate, there is annihilation.

The *Prajna Paramatia Heart Sutra* says:

> Form is not different from emptiness,
> Emptiness is not different from form.
> Form is emptiness, and emptiness is form...
> All dharmas are empty phenomena,
> They do not arise, nor are they annihilated;
> They are neither sullied nor clean,
> They do not increase or decrease,
> Thus, within emptiness there is no form,
> No sensation, imagination, action, cognition,
> No eyes, ears, nose, or body,
> No color, sound, flavor, taste, or touch.

> There is no realm to be seen,
> Nor is there a realm to be recognized,
> No darkness... no suffering, desire, annihilation,
> Way. No wisdom, no attainment, because,
> there is nothing to be attained.

Professor Xiong Shili once pointed out that Buddhist philosophy[9]

> ...from the cosmological aspect absorbs all phenomena into the heart-mind. Thus, the three worlds (past, present, and future) exist only in the mind, and all Dharma exists only in cognition... The mind and reality depend upon each other for co-dependent origination. Each moment, new things are sprouting. Nothing is at standstill. Nothing is certain.

Therefore, Buddhism denies the substantial phenomenal world of true arising and annihilation. "Form is emptiness, emptiness is form." "All Dharma is false and empty, like a dream or a flame. The image that is seen is like the moon in the river or a reflection in the mirror." (*Shuo Wugou Chengjing, Shengwen Pin*). "All sorts of phenomena are empty" (*Dazhi Du Lun*, Vol. XLIII). Everything in the phenomenal world is illusory. It neither exists nor non-exists.

When the Chinese aesthetic scholars of ancient times discussed the "aesthetic realm," they were obviously inspired by the "empty realm" of Buddhism. They hold thay because the artistic realm is a spiritual product that combines the artist's mind and objective phenomena, and therefore it's nature is a kind of image in the mind. This kind of image in the mind is what the artist gains from objective phenomena. It also becomes "cast" in the artist's mind. Therefore it has a double nature: 1) it is empty as well as real, and 2) it combines emptiness and reality. This is to say that the mental image is neither separated from conceptualized objective phenomena, nor totally a part of it. On the one hand it is a concrete, vivid, visible, and fragrant image. On the other, it is not a real substance that can be grasped. It is the combination of emptiness and substance that is "visible but beyond reach." (Si Kongtu, *Yuji Pushu*, quoting the words of Dai Yongzhou) From the modern aesthetic veiwpoint, it reflects the truth, but does not reduplicate it. It is only a kind of "illusion of reality," i.e., a kind of "created world." It cannot be seen as "being one with the ontic character of the phenomenon of reality." (I.e., the poetic image reflects but is not the same sort of reality as the external world). Nor can it be seen as "without realistic characteristics." It is "the extension of reality," but is not non-reality either.

What we would like to mention here in passing is that for a certain period of time, the world of Chinese aesthetic scholars oversimplified the characteristics of the term "realm." They held that realm is a mutual combination of thought and setting. The former is the content, while the latter is the form. Therefore realm is the unification of content and form. This kind of idea is aeons away from understanding the true characteristics of realm. Its greatest shortcoming is that it fails to understand the blend of emptiness and reality in realm.

Jiao Ran was the earliest example of explaining the dual nature of emptiness and reality by using the Buddhist concept of realm:

> Realm and setting are not one. Emptiness and reality are hard to distinguish. Scenery is visible but beyond reach. The wind is fragrant, but invisible. The mind manifests itself as "ego." It is functional, but non-substantial. Form is found in all phenomena, without its own material nature. All of this can be empty and real. (*Shiyi*)

Obviously the scenery which Jiao Ran called "visible but beyond reach," is not the objective material setting. Rather it is the "phenomenal image in the artistic realm." (i.e., what he called *jingxiang*, the imaginary realm). Therefore he also said that the "image" and "phenomena" contained in realm can only be a "mental picture," which sometimes is empty and sometimes is true. Because it "manifests itself as ego, it is functional but non-substantial," "Form is found in all phenomena, with no definite material nature." Therefore it exists in the time and space of imagination. It is the combination of emptiness and reality that is "visible and beyond reach." Because this kind of "mental picture" is a combination of emptiness and reality, which has a fertile and inspiring asthetic nature, it leads the reader into a realm of limitless imagination. Reality gives the realm a distinct image. Emptiness contains limitless implications, and leaves room for imagination.

Based on this kind of understanding, Jiao Ran creatively combined image with simile and metaphor, and proposed:

> Take the image for simile, and meaning for metaphor. I.e., meaning is subordinate to image. Every aspect of the myriad phenomena, birds, fish, grass, wood, and humans are all of a kind in metaphor and simile. (*Shishi*)

Again he says, "Metaphor makes the image present" (*Shiyi*). He has a fairly clear knowledge of the nature of image in the artistic realm, and the unlimited aesthetic imagination.

During the Sung Dynasty Yan Yu used *Chan* to explain poetry, as a way of eliciting inspiration:

> At the height of the Tang period, poetry was a matter of inspiration. The antelope left its horns, and ran off with no trace. Its most exquisite and delicate expressions cannot be borrowed or imitated, like sound echoing in the sky, the colors in things, the moon in the river, or a reflection in the mirror. The meaning goes beyond the limit of words.
> (*Canglang Shihua*)

What he expressed here was the aesthetic characteristics of poetry during the Tang Dynasty. Compared with Jiao Ran, Yan Yu's description of the nature of realm was more succinct and life-like. In the past quite a few authors criticized Yan Yu for introducing Buddhist ideas to make his expressions more mystical. In fact, a person familiar with the metaphors of Buddhism would judge his expressions to be more appropriate. He laid bare the basic nature of poetry, i.e., the internal aesthetic characteristics of the poetic realm.

From Yan Yu's point of view, the poetry of the Tang Dynasty expressed a kind of enthusiasm. This kind of passion mixed with external things as totally as water with milk. Both together became one substance, like the antelope that hung up his horns and disappeared without trace. What he used here was the metaphor employed by the Chan masters. A legend says that when antelopes sleep at night, they lift up feet from the earth by hanging themselves with their horns from a tree. Thus not even hounds can find any trace of them. In the *Sayings of Chan Masters*, this story is often used to illustrate the sudden enlightenment that goes beyond the meaning of words. For instance, the Chan master Xue Feng said:

> When I am rambling, you can still follow my words and sentences. But if I hang up my horns, where can you find my traces? (*Wudeng Huiyuan*, Vol. VII)

As another example, the Chan master Tao Ying once said:

> Like a good hunting dog, they are only good at finding footprints. But when they run across antelopes, they can't even smell them, let alone find their footprints. (*Wudeng Huiyuan*, Vol. X)

The other four similes, "sound echoing in the sky, the colors in things, the moon in the river, or a reflection in the mirror," are also often used in Buddhist scriptures to illustrate how the object is hard to pin down, and its true nature hard to discover. Yan Yu felt that the artistic realm that comes from passion is exactly this kind of a combination of the empty and real that I leaves no traces. Its meaning transcends the limitation of words. The word can be grasped, but the meaning is limitless. The artistic realm extends far beyond word. It manifests itself in the word, but goes beyond it. This is the special quality of the real and the empty in the artistic realm. It is the highest form of unification of image, passion, and limitless artistic feeling.

Following the development of the joining of poetry and Chan, after the Sung and Yuan Dynasties, scholars became more and more accustomed to using the special qualities of emptiness and reality to talk about the realm in poetry. For example:

> In poetry, the link with Chan is the use of words, when passion is one with movement. Chan is beyond the dust of the world, while movement is within it. It is as if it were seemingly there and not there. In this is where beauty itself resides. Those who understand this, can attain to what is subtly elegant. (Ming, Tang Xianzu, *Ru Lan Yi Ji Xu*)

> The two main points of writing poetry are style of tone, and the spiritual image. The tone and style are concrete, but there is no tangible spirit... take the flower in the mirror, and the moon on the water, as examples. Tone and style are the water and the mirror, while the flower and the moon are the spiritual image. Water and mirror must be clear; only then can the flower and moon be clear. (Ming, Hu Yinglin, *Shi Sou*, *Neibian*, Vol. 5)

> The most valuable part of poetry is that the meaning is crystal clear. It does not favor muddy or turbid truth, like a moon in the river and a reflection in the mirror that would be difficult to conceptualize... If the words are too realistic, then it lacks in flavor. If the feelings are too straight and rigid, then its hard to make thing move. So an image is required, which, when the reader thinks about it, he can almost taste it; moved, he becomes one with it. Distance and depth, this is the apogee of poetry. (Ming, Wang Tingxiang, *Yu Zheng Jiafu Xueshi Lun Shi Shu*)

> Poetry plumbs the depths of darkness and light. Looked at, its colors cannot be seen. Listened to, its sound cannot be heard. Far-reaching, but its image cannot be grasped.

It is subtle and circuitous, quiet and yet lively, empty, and yet real... Thus poetry reflects the heart-mind. (Qing, Wang Fuzhi, *Shiguang Juan*, Vol. V)

The apogee of poetry is limitless content. The subtlety of images falls in between what can and cannot be enunciated. That which it points to and to which it returns lies between the known and unknown. The words are here, but the meaning is there. It eliminates details and form, cuts away words and thoughts, leads the reader into the realm of deep profundity. Thus does it reach its apogee. (Qing, Ye Xie, *Yuan Shi*, *Nei Pian*)

Tang Xianzu compares the realm of Chan and poetry. He holds that both of them elaborate the formless and shapeless heart-mind with the reflections of phenomenal image. Therefore both of them take being and non-being as beautiful. He thinks very highly of the realm of being and non-being. Only by understanding this point can one understand poetry. What Hu Yinglin called spiritual image is another way of saying "realm." He held that the spiritual image in poetry, like the flower in the mirror and the moon in the river, is the "non-being and non non-being" combination of the empty and the real. Wang Tingxiang looks at it from the double nature of emptiness and reality in concpetual imagery. He holds that the "realm" in poetry is hard to be conceptualized. If one judge the real with the real, then it is "without flavor," and "hard to make things move." The realm in poetry should leave room for the reader to imagine and taste. He also regards the combination of the empty and the real as an important condition for the aesthetic birth and growth of the poetic realm.

Wang Fuzhi regards the double nature of the poetic realm to be a reflecion of the mind-heart of the artist. But, the reflections of the mind must have both image and reality. However, it is only a sort of "mental image." It is in between "darkness and light, empty and real," a seeming existence and seeming non-existence.

Therefore when Wang Fuzhi discussed the relationship between emotions and setting, he emphasized that the feelings must enter the setting, and the setting must partake of the feelings. In fact it means that the real must enter into the empty, thus making the real and empty one. Therefore it reaches the limitless blend of emotion and setting, which is the apogee of the poetic realm.

The aesthetic thought of Ye Xie is also influenced by Buddhism. He recognized that the realm of poetry lies in between the spoken and unspoken, the known and unknown. It

> ...reaches the outer limits of emptiness, which becomes the real, and the very outer reaches of distance, which become presence... it leaves room for the imagination.

When the reader uses the imagination to understand it, they can:

> Become one with the image, are moved by eyes, and understand through the heart-mind. (*Yuan Shi, Nei Pian*)

He also suggested the double nature of the combination of the empty and real in realm.

The aesthetics theory of ancient Chinese painting, in terms of the combination of the empty and real, received the deepest Buddhist influence. When the ancient painter and scholars of painting theory discussed the relationship between empty and filled spaces of the painting, (in fact, this concerns the creation of "realm" in painting) often borrowed the concept of "Form is emptiness, emptiness is form," from Buddhism. They used this style of thinking to create and criticize. Li Rihua of the Ming Dynasty said in his *Zizhu Xuan Za Zhui*:

> There are three levels of painting. The first is where the body is. In all places where body is, there is either closeness, or spaciousness. By the water or under the tree is where scenery is to be found. The second is where the eye rests. It is splendid scenery or deep mystery, such as water falling, clouds floating, sails moving, and birds flying. The third is where the mind wanders. It is where the vision stops, but the feelings continue. Tthere are such

> places where the mind is left behind. In drawing a tree
> or a stone, there must be a touch of grass. When depicting
> a vast scene, there must be places touched by the mind and
> absorbed by the spirit, where brush cannot reach. So, too,
> unless mind overlooks it, nothing would be overlooked.
> This is what Buddhism calls "The absolute distant form,
> and the absolute subtle form."

Here Li Zihua gives a detailed discussion of the relationship between the empty and the real in painting, especially the aesthetic value of emptiness, by dividing them into three levels. The body resides in the closest scenery. More realistic scenery shuld be placed here, while still paying attention to the combination of intensity and spaciousness. The eye rests in distant scenery, where there appears to be more emptiness and haziness. The mind wanders to vast scenery, which usually turns out to be the "emptiness" in the painting. The mind reaches where the brush failed to reach. But the emotions or feelings are continuous. Such places without color or form are filled out with mind. In Buddhist terms, it is the absolute distant form, and the absolute subtle form. The limitless is the absolute distant form, and the the most delicate is the absolute subtle form. Both of them refer to the form of "empty realm." They are formless and invisible. One can only comprehend it through consciousness.

There were many discussions during the Qing Dynasty about the combination of the empty and the real in painting. Among these, there were quite a few extensions and adaptations from Buddhist theory. For example Hua Lin pointed out in his *Nanzhong Juemi*: (*Ed. note*, quoting the Heart Sutra)

> The Chan masters said, "Form is no different from
> emptiness, and emptiness is not different from form. Form
> is emptiness, and emptiness is form." This explains the very
> truth of painting, i.e., the picture within the picture, and
> the picture outside the picture.
>
> White is the whiteness of paper. The side of all moun-

tains and stones facing the sun, smooth stone slopes, wide spaces of water and sky outside the painting, the empty and bright places of clouds and things, shadows at the foot of mountains, and the tops of trees, all of these are used to delineate the sky, water, smoke, clouds, roads, and sunlight are the same white. This kind of white is a color that the *maobi* calligraphers brush and the ink cannot depict. It is white within the painting, not the white of the paper. It has the touch of feeling. Otherwise, there would be no life in the painting. White is pure white, black is pure black. They do not match, yet they match. The white leaves comparatively more room for conception.

Hua Lin holds that the white in the paintings, even though it cannot be depicted by brush and ink, is still a part of the picture, or a part that is outside of the picture. Without it, the picture has not life. With it, there is more flavor. Pure white and pure black, scattered over the painting, seem to be a mismatch, but in fact best fits the aesthetic principle of painting. Looking at it from this point, white is black, and black is white. Both of them are the "picture within a picture." "Measure the black by the white, is the characteristic aesthetic principle of Chinese painters. It is quite different from the principles of painting used by their western counterparts.

Western aesthetic scholars very much admire this kind of oriental artistic idea of measuring the black with white. For example, the modern German aesthetic scholar Henry Lassiler said:[10]

> ...The white on the canvas glitters constantly, taking part in the role of effecting the whole work forcefully. What is more importan than person is nature. What is more important than nature are the various elements. What is more important than the elements is the empty white which is fundamental. Everything comes out from this empty white, and ends in it.

128

The above mentioned theory illustrates the artistic function of empty whiteness. The birth of "realm" in painting is caused by the co-origination of empty and real, and the combination of black and white.

In the Qing dynasty there were many scholars of art theory who held the same point of view as Hua Lin. For example, Daixi said, "The picture is where the brush and ink coalesce, but the delicacy of the picture is where brush and ink are absent." (*Xi Ku Jai Huaxu*). Da Chongguang said, "The co-origination of the empty and the real brings delicacy to the unpainted sections of the picture." (*Hua Chuan*). Fan Xun said,

> Painters of old knew how to use the brush to draw the empty and real in a wondrous fashion. What is called "the Way of painting" lies between the empty and the real. The empty and the real give the brush vividness and life. What is born from life is endless. (*Shanjingju Hualun*)

Zheng Ji holds that the essential matter of painting is the combination of empty and real. He said: "The secret of birth and change is 'empty empty, real real; real real, empty empty.' The eight words reveal all." (*Menghuanju Huaxue Jianming*) When the Qing scholars of the theory of painting discussed empty whiteness, even though they started from discussing the way of painting, in the end, all of them were concerned about the "realm" in painting. They thought that the essential character of the realm of painting lies in the co-origination of the empty and the real.

Zhong Baihua once said in his article, *The birth of the realm of Chinese art*:[11]

> The creation and formation of the realm of Chinese art needs 1) the sentimental passion of Qu Yuan, and 2) the detached free spirit of Zhuangzi (Chuang-tzu). With sentiment one can have passion and enter into the core of the myriad creature. This is called "being centered." With the aloof free spirit, one can transcend the phenomenal image (*Chaoyi xiangwai*), like the flower in the mirror, the

moon in the river, the antelope hanging its horns in a tree, leaving no trace to be found. "Form is emptiness, emptiness is form. Form is no different from emptiness, and emptiness is no different from form." This is not only the poetic realm of the Tang dynasty, but also the realm of painting of the Song and Yuan Dynasties.

After the later Tang period, the thought of Zhuangzi and Chan Buddhism mutually interpenetrated each other. When "the mutual gestation of existence and non-existence" of Taoism, and the "non-differentiation between form and and emptiness" of Buddhism manifest themselves in the realm of poetry and painting, there are hard to distinguish from each other.

III

What is closely conected with the combination of the empty and the real in realm is, "the scenery that is beyond the visible scenery, phenomena beyond phenomena, and flavor beyond flavor." Artists of ancient times regarded these criteria as the highest ideal of art. The aesthetic scholar of ancient times also regarded them as an ideal artistic realm, to evaluate and measure works of art by.

The discussion about scenery beyond scenery, phenomena beyond phenomena, and flavor beyond flavor started in the Six Dynasties. At that time the Neo Taoist (Xuanxue) philosophers talked glibly about the relationship between words, realm, and phenomena. Under the disguise of talking about the Book of Change, Laozi (Lao-tzu), and Zhuangzi (Chuang-tzu), Xun Can was the first scholar who suggested the issue of "beyond phenomena." According to the glosses of the *San Guo Zhi*, the *Weishu*, section, *Xun Yu Zhuan*, quoting He Shao's *Xun Can Zhuan*:

> Respected friends of Xun Can, who were fond of talking about Confucianism, and Xun Can himself who was very

interested in Taoism, always felt that Zigong thought that Confucius' idea about Nature and Heaven's way, was not reccorded. Thus even though the six books are preserved, they are only the chaff and husks of the sages. One of his friends named Yu once challenged him, saying: "The Sages set up images in the Book of Changes to show its meaning. All of these were done by words. Then why say that subtleties cannot be attained by words, yet seen and heard?" Can answered, "Subtle reasoning is not grasped by the image of things. Just now you said that the model is set up to illustrate the meaning. It does not go beyond reasoning, but is a manner of using words. It is not the words, but the surface only. Since the surface of words was used to discuss what is beyond phenomena, the hidden meaning could not come forth.

Xun Can thought that it was by setting up images that the sages illustrated meaning in the Book of Changes, and that the subtlety of the concepts could not be completely contained in phenomenal images. Therefore there was a meaning beyond phenomena. Wang Bi, in his book *Zhoyi Lueli*, the *Mingxiang* chapter, also carefully illustrated the idea of getting the image and throwing away the words, getting the meaning and throwing away the image:

> Image gives birth to idea; words make the image clear. Nothing other than image can fulfill idea; nothing other than word can clarify image. Words come from image; thus one can follow the words to observe the image. Image is born from idea. Therefore, one can follow the image to observe meaning. Meaning can reveal itself by image, and image can manifest itself by words. Thus, words make image clear. Once image is grasped, one can throw away words. Meaning is conceived in image. Once meaning is grasped, one can throw away the image... Therefore, those who hold onto the words cannot obtain the image, while

those who hold onto the image, cannot grasp the meaning. What is preserved in an image born from meaning is not the same image anymore. What is preserved in a word born from image is not the same word anymore. Those who forget the image get the meaning; those who forget words get the image. By forgetting the image, meaning is grasped. By forgetting the word, image is won. Therefore, image illustrates meaning, and yet the image itself can be forgotten. The picture is drawn to express passion, and yet the picture itself can be forgotten.

In the confluence and mutual usage of Neo-Taoism (Xuanxue) and Buddhism, Buddhists of the Six Dynasties also used the term *xiangwai* "beyond phenomena" to illustrate that the highest truths of Buddhism cannot be passed on by words, and the *Dharma Laksana* realm of Buddha cannot be visualized. The Realm of Nirvana (Buddhism holds that this is the highest and most ideal of all realms) transcends form and image. E.g., Seng Zhao holds:

> Sacred wisdom (i.e., the wisdom of Buddha, i.e., the *zhen di* Paramartha, the truths of Buddhism), in its subtlety, is deep and hidden, difficult to fathom. It has no image, no name, and cannot be obtained by word or image.
>
> (*Panruo Wuzhi Lun*)

To realize the non-phenomenal *Paramartha* Buddhist Truths, one must have extraordinary *shenming* spiritual insight to penetrate and grasp their meaning. This is the "non-knowledge" wisdom of the sages, whereby they can have "non knowledge that knows of itself, non act that acts of itself." (Ibid.) This "non-knowledge" is a kind of intuition not based on rational (deductive) thinking. It looks as if nothing is known, but in fact everything is known. He (Seng Zhao) held that "this can reach the highest spiritual wisdom, and goes beyond discussing the phenomenal." (Ibid.) Only by possessing this kind of wisdom of non-knowing in which nothing is not known, can one reach the highest spiritual wisdom, and understand the truth that transcends phenomenal image.

Another example is Zhu Daosheng, who holds that:

> The perfect image is without form, and perfect sound is without noise. How in the subtle and speculative realm can there be form and words? (*Miaofa Lianhua Jingshu, Shupin*).

This highest truth and wondrous Dharma that transcends sound, word, form, and image, how can one probe and grasp it? Daosheng, after thinking it over, finally reached the "wise conclusion" that total enlightenment is beyond words, and forgetting the word gets the idea. He said,

> Image is used to illustrate meaning. When the meaning is grasped, image is forgotten. Words are used to elaborate the meaning. Once meaning is elaborated, they disappear... When the fish is caught, the net is forgotten. Only then can we speak with words. (*Gaoseng Zhuan, Zhu Daosheng Zhuan*)

Again he said:

> Image is where meaning dwells. To hold onto image is to be confused by the meaning. Conversion is the goal of preaching. To be caught up in preaching restricts conversion. To be absorbed in words and the real, to be lost in empty absurdity, to seek with the mind in responding to things, is to be lost and blind.

(The preface of Huilin's *Longguang Si Zhu Daosheng Fashi Lei*; see *Guanghong Mingji*, Vol. XXIII).

Daosheng felt that phenomena are false images of Buddhist truth. By no means can one rely upon them inflexibly. One must get the meaning, and then forget the image. I.e., what one must really get is the meaning beyond the image. Daosheng's theory was deeply colored and influenced by Zhuangzi and Neo-Taoism. His manner of thinking was basically the same as that of

Laozi and Zhuangzi. But by reason of his intelligence, he adapted the manner of thinking of Laozi and Zhuangzi to be assimilated to that of Buddhism. In the *Weimuo Jijing* (Vimalakirti Sutra), which was translated by that time, there were also records of the Vimalakirti way of thinking, i.e., the "quietness without words." Manjusri asked Vimalakirti:

> We speak of it relatively. The benevolent must say,
> What is meant by "The Boddhisattva enters the one and only Dharma gate?"

Vimalakirti answered:

> Quietness without words.
> Manjusri applauded:
> Great! Marvelous! To reach the ultimate
> where there are no words or language,
> Is to reach the ultimate Dharma gate!
> (*Vimalakirti Sutra*, *Ru Bu Er Famen Pin*)

The Vimalakirti Sutra, which was translated by Kumarajiva, recorded Vimalakirti's words:

> All of the Dharmas are like illusory phenomena. So, you shouldn't be afraid of anything. Why? All that is spoken is not distinct from phenomena. As for the wise, they do not rely on words; therefore, they do not have fear. Why is this so? Words are distinct from nature. Without words there is liberation.

Buddhism holds that words are used when there is no other recourse. Therefore it is "distinct from nature." From the Buddhist viewpoint, "The working of the mind must be extinguished, the speaking of words must be terminated." Daosheng's "wise conclusion" was born from and stimulated by Buddhism. Therefore it is very difficult to say that the manner of thinking of Daosheng belongs purely to Zhuangzi, Neo-Taoism or Buddhism. After Daosheng, Hui Jiao, the author of the *Gaoseng Zhuan* also said:

> Ultimate truth is without words. The ultimate mystery

is deep and abstruse. Because of its depth and obscurity, "the workings of the mind must be cut off; without words, speaking is terminated... Therefore the deep abyss must first be reached, and then wonders beyond words attained.
(*Gaoseng Zhuan*, *Yijie Lun*)

We can see that in the Six Dynasties there were quite a few discussions about "beyond phenomena," "beyond words" in Buddhist circles.

Neo-Taoism, as a way of thinking, also penetrated into the realm of art and aesthetics, together with the Buddhist idea of "beyond phenomena, beyond words." During the Six Dynasties the concept of "beyond phenomena" had already appeared in the aesthetic theory of painting. For example, when Xie He critiqued Zhang Mo and Xun Xu in his *Guhua Pinlu*, said:

The style and atmosphere is delicate and spiritual, when the subtle essence is taken away, skeleton and bones cast out. If confined by the physical object, the quintessence is absent. When one gets beyond phenomena, the surface is tiring. This is wherein wondrous subtlety lies.

Xie He believes that to understand the style and atmosphere of the paintings of Zhang Mo and Xun Xu, one must not only hold onto the physical objective, but rather one should see what is beyond. It is only from beyond that one can detect the subtle. It could be said that Xie He's explanation is the first echo in aesthetic theory of the Neo-Taoist idea that "words cannot complete meaning," and its Buddhist counterparts, i.e., "the speaking of words is terminated" and "holding the discussion beyond phenomena."

Zhong Bing in his *Hua Shan Shui Xu* is also concerned about the "beyond phenomena" problem. He said:

The thinking that came to an end in medieval times, can be found 1,000 years later. As for the subtle that is beyond words and image, can it be culled from within books?

In literary theory, even though the *Wenxin Diaolong* of Liu Xie did not use the word "beyond phenomena," in fact, he discussed this problem too. In the chapter *Shensi Pian* he said:

> The idea comes from thinking, and words come from the idea. When dense, no limit; when sparse, they are vast. Reason confined to a square inch, is probed in vastness; Meaning may be a foot away, but thinking roams beyond rivers and mountains.

This is similar to Xie He's idea of "culled from far beyond phenomena," and Zong Bing's "The most subtle is beyond words and image." In the same context he mentioned that the delicacy of art work cannot be reached by words. In the *Yinxiu Pian* chapter he said, "What is hidden is most important outside the literary work." "The hidden gives importance to double meaning." Going one step further, he explained:

> The hidden is the essential, the meaning is external. The secret is opened obliquely. A buried seed grows unseen just as the single lines of the trigrams (in the *Yijing*) are mutually changed into each other, like pearl and jade hidden in the river. Therefore the mutual changes of the trigrams show the four seasons. Pearl and jade submerged in water send ripples outward.

He thinks the "hidden" (equivalent to a category in aesthetics called the "implicit") has multiple meanings, that are usually outside of literary works, and have the nature of limitless growth. They are just like the never ending changes of the Trigrams (in the *Yijing*). They are also like pearl and jade under the water. The brilliance glows and radiates under the surface of the water. This kind of "hidden" quality can produce an after taste of artistic beauty. Concepts such as "beyond phenomena," "outside of literature," and "after taste," from the aesthetic world of the Six Dynasties laid a good foundation for the theory of "ideal realm" in later generations.

After the mid-Tang dynasty, the rise and flourishing of Chan Buddhism went a step further in developing the "get the meaning, forget the image," and "not relying on words" thought of Neo-Taoism and Buddhism in the Six Dynasties, and took it as its own idea. The Sixth Patriarch Hui Neng, laid great importance on awakening to one's own (Buddha) nature from within. His method was immediate enlightenment, which did not rely on words. He said, "If one relies on words in various Buddhist texts, the meaning of the Buddha cannot be attained." (Song Zanning, *Xu Gaoseng Zhuan, Hui Neng Zhuan*). Some of the Chan masters also advocated that:

> One cannot grasp the meaning by turning to words, paper, and ink...
> Confusion is found in words, enlightenment in the heart...
> Those who get the meaning jump over superficial words;
> Those who grasp *Li* reasoning, go beyond language.
> (*Da Zhu Chan Shi Yulu*, Vol. II)
> Buddha is the work of mind. How can one seek it in words.
> *Junzhou Huang Nie Duanji Chanshi Chuanxin Fayao*)

Yet others thought that Buddhist truth cannot be expressed in words. If one still wants to try, then, "once (the word) touches the lips, the meaning is lost." (*Wudeng Huiyuan*, Vol. XII)

Liu Yuxi of the Tang Dynasty first suggested the presupposition that "realm is born outside of phenomena." This is the first time that realm was linked with what is beyond phenomena. Jiao Ran also mentioned many times the importance of "beyond phenomena" and "forgetting phenomena" in the realm of thought. He said:

> Take the wondrous from beyond phenomena; portray the lively from what flies and moves; describe the true mysteries of thought. (*Shi Yi*)

He said in another place, "See the meaning in image." (*Shi Shi*)
He also discussed the problems of purpose outside of literary
work. He held that the "multiple nature of meaning lies outside
literary work," (i.e., has multi-layered meaning).

> Seeing nature while ignoring words is the ultimate way of poetry. (*Shih Shih*)

Si Kongtu of the Late Tang period mixed together Buddhist and Taoist ideas, and even more clearly suggested the concept of ideal realm as a "image outside of phenomena," and "scenery beyond scenery." What he pursued was the unification of internal image and external phenomena. This too brought about the unification of the empty and the real, form and spirit, the limited and the limitless. What was meant by saying "don't rely on a single word, to grasp the feeling and atmosphere," was not to completely throw off words. Instead, it meant not to cling to words. This is similar to what the Chan masters believed, " not to cling to the false, but to awaken to what is beyond phenomena.

Si Kongtu's theory of the ideal realm had a deep influence on later generations. Neither Yan Yu's theory of enthusiasm, nor Wang Shizhen's "romantic charm" surpassed the theoretical sphere defined by Si Kongtu. From the aspect of connotation, his ideas are much clearer than Yan Yu or Wang Shizhen. But from the aspect of conrete illustration, Yan Yu and Wang Shizhen were more influenced by the Chan school.

In conclusion, the theory of realm belongs to a category of aesthetics, which is one of the most representative characteristics of Chinese art. In its philosophical sources, there are Confucian, Taoist, and Buddhist texts. In its birth and historical development, Buddhism and Daoism were its gestators. Its main theoretical point of view and manner of thought was drawn out and transformed by the Buddhist theory of realm, which had a deep and lasting effect on all subsequent forms of Chinese art.

REFERENCES

I. Notes of Ren Jiyu

1. See "A Forward to the Dunhang manuscript of the Platform Sutra," (Tan Jing), in Symposium of the National Dunhuang Academic Conference, Lanzhou: Gansu People's Press, 1983.
2. Lunjiashizi Ji (Records of Masters of the Lankavatara Sutra, Sung,Gaoseng zhuan, (Biographies of Eminent Monks compiled during the Song Period), Song Dynastic History, Ch. 8. Also, Jingde Chuandenglu (Records of Transmission of the Lamp, compiled during the Jingde period, 1104-07), Ch. 4.
3. Lunjia Shizi Ji, Ch. 8. (Qu Qu Zhi, bend the crooked straight).
4. See: Beizong Wu Fangbian Men (The Five Upaya of the Northern Chan school), Dacheng Beizong Lun (On the Mahayana of Northern Chan), Dacheng Wu Fangbian (The Five Upaya of Mahayana), the Bodhidharma Guan Xin Lun, Jue Guan Lun, etc,.
5. Wu Xin Lun, under the title Shi Puti Damo Zhi, (An explanation of Bodhidharma's rules). Cf. Dunhuang, S. 296.
6. This passage from the Dacheng Beizhong Lun cited in Note 4 above, is also found in Dazhang Jing, Vol. 85, p. 1282.
7. Dazhang Jing, Vol. 82, p. 1282.
8. Dazhang Jing, Vol. 85, p. 1270. Dunhuang Mss. S. 296.
9. Ibid.
10. Jue Guan Lun, Strophe 6.
11. Ibid.
12. Dharma Guan Xin Lun. Dunhuang Ms. edit.
13. Dunhuang Mss., Guan Xin Lun, Intro.
14. See Wen Yucheng, "The Transmission of the Northern Chan School," in Shijie Zongjiao Yanjiu (Studies on World Religion), Vol. II, 1983, No. 2.
15. Song Gaoseng Zhuan, Ch. 11.
16. Song Gaoseng Zhuan, Ch. 9.

II. Notes of Du Jiwen

1. There are three kinds of Buddhism in modern China: 1) Buddhism that uses Chinese language as a medium, 2) Tibetan Buddhism, and 3) southern or Theravada Buddhism found in Yunnan and other southern provinces. We limit ourselves in this article to Chinese Buddhism up until the end of the Sui-T'ang period.
2. Zami, Tantric Buddhist texts, see the Taisho Buddhist Canon, Vols. 18-21.
3. Xiaocheng (Hinayana) is translated here as Theravada-Nikaya, rather than "Lesser Vehicle," in keeping with modern scholarly usage.
4. A branch of Vaibhasika, said to have been founded by Rahul.
5. Yichieh you.
6. Geng Sheng Lun.
7. Naxian Biqiu Jing.
8. I.e., the Sarvastivadins, Vaibhasika, and their eventual offshoots, the Sautantrikas and Mulasarvastivadins; ed. note.
9. Yao-Qin shi de Guan Ho Jiu Shuo.
10. Wei Muo Chie Jing.
11. Muo Jie.
12. Wulian Shou Jing.
13. Liudu Ji Jing.
14. Hou Han Ji, by the E. Jin scholar Yuan Hong.
15. Hou Han Shu, Xiyu Juan.
16. Yan Shi Jia Shun, Guixin Pian.
17. Zhuangzi, Juan 2, Jaiwu Lun.
18. See Hung Ming Ji, Muozi Lihui Lun.
19. Ibid.
20. See the Ru Tao Jiu Liu, nine grades of Taoist orders.
21. See Fuozu Lidai Tongzai, Juan 30.
22. Yuan Dao Lun, quoted in Op. Cit., note 20 above.
23. Fang Guang Panluo Jing.
24. Sun Chao, Dao Xian Lun.
25. Kungqiao Wong Zhou, Pheasant King Mantra.
26. Ibid.

27. Ibid.

28. Da Yun Jing, Sheng Man Jing, for which latter see below, Srimala Sutra.

29. See Zhi Dun, Zhi Jie Lun Shu.

30. The Five Hu nationalities of the northern kingdoms were the Xiongnu, Jie, Zhi, Chiang, and Xianbei.

31. Da Ji Jing.

32. Da Panluo Jing.

33. Shidi Jing Lun.

34. Dapan Niheng Jing.

35. Sheng Man Jing.

36. Lengjia Jing.

37. Xie Dacheng Lun.

38. Xie Dacheng Lun.

39. Fahua Jing.

40. I.e., the Da Cheng, and Chengshi "All True" branch of Madhyamika, translated by Kumarajiva ca. 406 CE.

41. Cheng Weishi Lun.

42. Da Ci En Shih Sanzang Fashi Juan.

43. I.e., the Cheng Wei Shi Lun, Yogacara school of pure idealism.

44. Song Gao Seng Juan.

45. The Chinese version of the Vidya Matrasiddhi Sastra, reduced from Vasubandhu's original to ten fascicles in Chinese.

46. Jie Shenmi Jing Shu.

47. Huayan Jing, the Garland Sutra.

48. Bu Kong, Ren Wong Hu Guo Ching.

49. Hui Yuan, Shamen Bujing Wangje Lun.

50. Ibid.

51. Shihui Zhangju.

III. Notes of Cai Dahua

1. See Wen Yiduo, Zhuangzi Neipian Xiaoshi.

2. See Sijiao Yi Beishi, Ch. 1.

3. See Fazhang, Huayan Yicheng Jiaoyi Fenji Zhang.

4. Note that Buddhism uses three kinds of different effects to determine three kinds of original natures in humans: the person who listens to the doctrine, the one who awakens to the doctrine of causation, and the Bodhisattva. The text here refers to the first two kinds of nature.

5. See the Maha-prajnaparamita Sutra, Introduction: "If one wishes to use the way of the seed of wisdom to realize fully all forms of wisdom,... if one wishes to use all forms of wisdom to realize fully the seeds of every form of wisdom, it is necessary to put into practice the Prajnaparamita."

6. The Dazhidu Lun (Treatise on Crossing over to Mahamati the Shore of Great Wisdom), a Sastra ascribed to Nagarjuna, translated by Kumarajiva, 397-415 CE.,Juan 27.

7. Fuozu Tongji, Juan 6, Erzu Bei Qi Zunzhe Huiwen Benji.

8. From the Zhonglun Madhyamika text of Nagarjuna, "The Chapter on Contemplating the Four Noble Truths."

9. Note the Buddhist use of "fragrance" (gandha) or incense through the sense of smell to stimulate faith and devotion; W.E. Soothill, A Dictionary of Chinese Buddhist Terms, Oxford: 1934, p. 318.

10. Sanshi has a variety of meanings, the most common of which is "past, present, and future. The meaning assigned here comes from the Mahamatri (Dazhi Du Lun), a sastra ascribed to Nagarjuna on the Maha-Prajnaparamita Sutra, translated by Kumarajiva into 100 Juan between 397-415 CE.

11. See the Dacheng Qixin Lun kao zheng (A Critical edition of the Mahayana Awakening of Faith Sastra).

12. The passage here is close to Zhuangzi's notions of "Tao... derives from its own source, its own roots" (Ch. 6), and "There is no place in which Tao is not" Ch. 22).

13. See Fazang, Yicheng Jiaoyi Fenji Zhang (Chapter on the Meaning and Divisions of the Ekayana).

14. Huayan Jing, Shenxuan Ji, Juan 1.

15. Huayan Yicheng Jiaoyi Fenji Zhang, Juan 4.

16. See the Sung Gaozeng Juan, (Sung Dynasty Record of Famous Monks), Juan 8,

17. Mazu Daoyi, founder of the independent "Southern Peak" school of southern Chan Buddhism, (in Jiangxi province).

18. The text here reads shi corpse, or in the funeral rite, the heir to the dead master of the household. Thus Wu-Wei is both "dead," i.e., unmoving, un-revived, and master of the Taoist's life.

IV. Notes of Jiang Shuzhuo

1. See: Lü Zhi, Zhongguo Fuoxue Yuanliu Luejiang, Zhonghua Press, 1979, pp. 119-20.
2. Ding Fubao, Fuaxue Da Cidian, Wenwu Press, 1984, p. 1247.
3. Fuoxue Da Cidian, p. 804.
4. Xiung Shili, Fuojia Mingxiang Tongshi, The Chinese Encylopedia Press, 1985, p. 9.
5. Shi Cun, Yinming Yaoshu, Zhonghua Press, 1986, p. 121.
6. Op. Cit., p. 120.
7. The quotation of the Shige here is taken from the version found in the Wenjing Mifu Lun.
8. See Lü Zhi, Zhongguo Fuoxue Yuanliu Luejiang, p. 181.
9. Xiong Shili, Fuojia Mingxiang Tongshi, p. 6.
10. Henry Lassiler, A Discussion of the Incomplete Nature of Art, quoting from Elissiyev, Art and World Religions, Chinese Version, Arts and Culture Press, 1989, p. 143.
11. Zong Baihua, Meixue Sanbu (Walking in Aesthetics), The Shanghai People's Press, 1981 edition, p. 65.